As It Is Written and Intended

As It Is Written and Intended

Living Scripture and Reading Life

JASON N. YUH

WIPF & STOCK · Eugene, Oregon

AS IT IS WRITTEN AND INTENDED
Living Scripture and Reading Life

Copyright © 2025 Jason N. Yuh. All rights reserved. Except for brief quotations in critical publications or reviews, no part of this book may be reproduced in any manner without prior written permission from the publisher. Write: Permissions, Wipf and Stock Publishers, 199 W. 8th Ave., Suite 3, Eugene, OR 97401.

Wipf & Stock
An Imprint of Wipf and Stock Publishers
199 W. 8th Ave., Suite 3
Eugene, OR 97401

www.wipfandstock.com

PAPERBACK ISBN: 979-8-3852-5042-4
HARDCOVER ISBN: 979-8-3852-5043-1
EBOOK ISBN: 979-8-3852-5044-8

Unless otherwise indicated, Scripture quotations are from the ESV® Bible (The Holy Bible, English Standard Version®), copyright © 2001 by Crossway, a publishing ministry of Good News Publishers. ESV Text Edition: 2025. Used by permission. All rights reserved.

All emphases in Scripture quotations have been added by the author.

"To read Scripture as centered on Christ is not to force him into the details of texts from which he is ostensibly absent. Instead, it is to see how Scripture reveals God's character, the plight of sinful humanity, and the role of God's people in such a way that the texts themselves establish trajectories culminating in Christ. *As it is Written and Intended* is a helpful, practical guide to interpreting biblical narratives in this way, leading us deeper into the witness of all of Scripture to Christ."

—STEPHEN CHESTER, Lord and Lady Coggan Professor of New Testament, Wycliffe College, University of Toronto

"This book will help you see how all of Scripture coheres in Christ, and what that means for your life."

—BRANDON D. CROWE, Professor of New Testament, Westminster Theological Seminary

"Jason writes with the heart and voice of a pastor. He offers several thoughtful principles for interpreting Scripture, but two are especially noteworthy. First, he underscores the vital distinction between the Creator and creation, an essential lens through which the entire Bible should be read. Second, he affirms that we see Christ in every part of Scripture. These insights reflect a theological conviction and pastoral sensitivity that will enrich a reader's engagement with God's word."

—PETER ROBINSON, Professor of Proclamation, Worship, and Ministry, Wycliffe College, University of Toronto

"To resist the rise of Moralistic Therapeutic Deism, the next generation must see Christ as central to both life and the world. This vision begins by recognizing him as the protagonist of Scripture and the lens through which we understand God's truth and the story of the world. *As It Is Written and Intended*, by Jason Yuh, offers a compelling, theologically rich guide to reclaiming this Christ-centered perspective in both Scripture and life."

—BILL DEJONG, Faculty Chaplain, Redeemer University, Ancaster, Ontario

"It has been rightly said that one important way of viewing the past two millennia of church history is as a dialogue with holy Scripture. And a critical part of that dialogue is how best to interpret the word of God. This fresh study of the hermeneutical task by a gifted biblical scholar, Jason Yuh, re-focuses our interpretative gaze on what must be central in any prolonged and deep reading of the Bible: Jesus Christ. Highly recommended!"

—MICHAEL A.G. AZAD HAYKIN, Professor of Church History, Southern Baptist Theological Seminary

Contents

Acknowledgments ix

Introduction: Living Scripture and Reading Life 1

Chapter 1: In the Beginning: Jesus Christ as the True Adam (Gen 1–3) 10

Chapter 2: Defining the Approach: CREATOR-Creature Distinction, the Problem of Sin, and the Organism of Scripture 27

Chapter 3: Christ as the True Israel (Exod 19–20, 24) 52

Chapter 4: Christ as the True David (Ruth 4, 1 Sam 16–17, 2 Sam 7) 80

Chapter 5: Christ as the Epitome of All Examples 112

Conclusion: From and To Christ 143

Appendix: The Writings and the Prophets 145

Glossary 151

Bibliography 153

Acknowledgments

I WANT TO THANK all the students, colleagues, congregation members, and others who have encouraged me to write this book, especially those who have raised questions and provided feedback. Some of these individuals include Avril Schatz, Bill DeJong, Brandon Crowe, David Fuller, Eden Corner, Emma Gringhuis, Esther Lee, Henry Lee, James Goobie, James Wood, Jennifer Suh, Jessica Joustra, Jina Lee, John Lee, Jonathan Schock, June Oh, Kevin Flatt, Lane Tipton, Michael Haykin, Michael Jung, Niki Florica, Owen Ecker, Rebekah Kwon, Richard Kim, Sally Han, Shirley Gim, Simon Mischuk, Tony Kim, and Tyrel Luchies. I also want to acknowledge that this publication would not be possible without the support and guidance of Wipf and Stock Publishers and Redeemer University. Lastly, I want to recognize the indispensable role that my family has played: Jeanie, Jude, Juliet, and Jubilee!

Introduction
Living Scripture and Reading Life

OVERVIEW

How we see Scripture directly correlates with how we see life. If we see Jesus Christ organically and meaningfully in every part of Scripture, then we will see him that way in every aspect of life. As lofty as that might sound, the inverse is also true: if we struggle to see Christ organically and meaningfully in various parts of Scripture, then we will struggle to see him that way in various aspects of life. The reality is that in many areas of life, we do not see the prominence of Christ organically and meaningfully. The relevance of Christ in a given situation might feel forced (so it is not organic) or superficial (so it is not meaningful). Consequently, we settle for a warped understanding of God's word, the gospel, and our life. This results in many of the symptoms that plague Christians, such as burnout, self-righteousness, or apathy.

A helpful way forward is to recognize that God has designed reality in a particular manner so that the way we engage in his word directly correlates with the way we engage our lives. All of life, especially his word, finds its true meaning, purpose, and fulfillment in Christ alone. It is of course difficult to live this way, so God's word is provided to reorient the way we see life. However, if we fail to see God's word as intended, then there is little hope that we will be able to live life as intended.

The purpose of this book is to help us engage in God's word so that we behold Christ in every part of both Scripture and life by offering an approach to Scripture that is from Scripture itself. Thus, the heart of this approach is to engage in God's word as he himself intends. The approach is introduced in the opening chapters of Genesis and developed in subsequent parts of Scripture. It is simple and accessible, yet profound and unfathomable—such tension is expected from God's word. Hence, the basic principles of this approach are somewhat truisms, yet they might not be understood in the flow of Scripture or applied consistently. To remedy this, the book provides "how-to" guides with complementary diagrams through key examples from Scripture so that we can truly understand the approach and employ it consistently. This will assist us in seeing that all of Scripture is grounded, saturated, and culminating in Christ alone; and in turn, we will see that all of life is grounded, saturated, and culminating in Christ alone.[1]

WHERE IS THE DEATH AND RESURRECTION OF CHRIST?

One of the motivations for writing this book is my experiences with both Scripture and the Christian life. Although these experiences have been quite diverse and full of joy, I noticed an underlying problem. Jesus Christ, particularly his death and resurrection, has not been sufficiently or consistently prominent.

Our Experience with Scripture

Ever since high school, I cherished my time in Scripture, even more than hanging out with friends or playing video games. I frequently looked forward to either being a part of a small group Bible study or leading one. Among my unexpected experiences with Scripture were the invaluable conversations I had with my coworkers while I was in software development. Most of them were atheists, yet they had incisive questions and challenging perspectives that motivated me to gain greater familiarity with some of the overlooked aspects of Scripture.

I read through Scripture from Genesis to Revelation at least twelve times before beginning seminary, and this interest evolved even further as I began and completed my doctoral studies as a biblical scholar specializing in the New Testament and early Christianity. Here I acquired proficiency in the biblical languages of Hebrew and Greek; expertise in many contexts of both the Old and New Testaments; and training in the academic theory and

---

1. In the words of Herman Bavinck, "All the revelations and words of God, in nature and history, in creation and re-creation, both in the Old and the New Testament, have their ground, unity, and center in him" *Reformed Dogmatics*, 1:402.

Introduction

method of religion, sociology, anthropology, and many other cognate areas of study. This resulted in a burst of research articles in the most selective scholarly journals of my fields.

The most impactful experience has been my role as a pastor. The church is ultimately entrusted with the word of God, so ministering the whole counsel of Scripture with exegetical discipline while organically and meaningfully showing Christ has been by far the most formative factor in my growth in Scripture. Moreover, this took place not merely behind the pulpit but in many forms: one-on-one conversations, small group discussions, lecture-style settings, and—most importantly—teaching children of all ages (if you can effectively teach children, then you can teach anyone!). What has made my role as a pastor so indispensable is that it compelled me to reflect upon how the average person perceives Scripture. This crystallized further through my experience as a professor of biblical studies, where I have the privilege of teaching both Old and New Testaments.

In summary, my experience with God's word has led me to diverse settings—from confessional institutions, to being trained to view the Bible with a secular approach, to having the privilege of teaching in ecclesial and academic roles. As much as I am thankful for these experiences, the reality is that we struggle to see Christ consistently preeminent in our engagement with his word.

Our "Christian" Life

The developments in my journey in God's word have coincided with those of my Christian life. In high school, my Christian life was almost exclusively fueled by the desire for intimacy in my relationship with God. I mostly measured my growth in Christ by eschewing immature practices, like cursing or being rude to others, and by acquiring "Christian" practices, like praying and reading the Bible. As an undergraduate, my life in Christ was more about having a sense of purpose or mission. Much of my identity as a Christian was based on how effective my ministry and influence on others were. Involvement in ministries were therefore critical for me. As a husband and a young father, the gauge was more sophisticated. Rather than focusing on actions or behavior, it was more about how theologically thoughtful my perspective on life was and the efficacy of my evangelism efforts to my coworkers and neighbors. Similar to my journey in God's word, my life as a Christian has brought a wide range of experiences and emphases. And likewise, I realize that so much of our Christian lives orbit around "good" things (e.g., our maturation, church community, etc.) rather than Christ—especially his death and resurrection.

The Problem

So despite my general appreciation for these diverse experiences, I noticed that the glory of Christ has not always been central. The gospel of Christ, for the most part, seems to be either in the background or reduced to the forgiveness of sins.[2] This belittling of the gospel begins with how our engagement with Scripture inconsistently points to Christ. Instead, we often treat Moses, David, Peter, or Paul as the main character rather than God. The consequences of this seemingly innocent misunderstanding are catastrophic. Scripture becomes merely another book for wise living, good morals, or self-help.[3] The sovereign God who is the CREATOR and sustainer of all things becomes small in our minds while the side characters become dominant. As a result, we mistake ourselves or those around us (e.g., our boss, spouse, children, etc.) as the main character while we relegate God to the background—a side character who is only summoned when we cannot fix the problem ourselves.

During the 2020 lockdown, I wrote that Scripture is primarily about God himself. Relatedly, Scripture exposes "the fragility, corruption, and misery of humanity." Thus, God's word repeatedly reminds us that "humanity does not merely require self-help books that provide practical steps for improvement or philosophical musings that explain away suffering. Humanity is in dire need of something outside of itself: a Savior."[4] However, often when we engage in Scripture, our main takeaway is to place the focus on ourselves—whether it is more actions that eventually burn us out or optimistic fluff that eventually leaves us dry.

Similarly, our Christian life frequently focuses more on being inspired toward a particular action, behavior, or mindset rather than magnifying the

---

2. Similarly, Richard B. Gaffin Jr. raises the question of whether we have reduced the gospel to only the righteousness of Christ rather than appreciating the fullness of Christ (*By Faith*, 109–10).

3. Other writers have also observed something similar: Gaffin writes that if we overlook the reality of the resurrection of Christ, then Christianity becomes merely "deadening moralism" (*By Faith*, 76); Christian Smith and Melinda Lundquist Denton have described this as "Therapeutic Moral Deism" (*Soul Searching*, 162–71).

4. Yuh, introduction to *Kingdom Manifesto*, x.

myriad depths of who Christ is and what he has done. When we do reflect upon the gospel, it is more about the benefits of the gospel rather than the person of the gospel. What can *we* get out of this rather than adoring Christ.

Consequently, our lives are essentially the same as any other sincere, well-intentioned individual who may have no regard for God, let alone Christ—there is no substantial difference between Christians and non-Christians other than a few superficial habits. Rarely are we aware of the gravity of our sin, and therefore seldomly are we overwhelmed by the richness of his grace. We perceive ourselves as mostly impervious to sin since we do not struggle with the main vices that have been defined by society.[5] Other than what our lips have been trained to say through catechism, we live our lives with the same joy, hope, or purpose that any other individual has. Our joy might be to make progress on our personal bucket lists or to foster meaningful relationships with others; or our hope is often financial security or living a life filled with pleasant memories; or our purpose is reduced to being morally decent individuals and courteous to others. In the way that we both live Scripture and read life, the emphasis is often on enhancing the self or the horizontal dynamics of interpersonal relationships. The gospel of Christ and humanism have become roughly synonymous. Of course, these emphases are virtuous, but there is nothing distinctively *Christ*ian about them.

How Scripture Summarizes Itself and the Christian Life

Scripture, however, makes bold claims about both itself and the Christian life. According to Christ, all of Scripture points to himself—especially his death and resurrection:

> Then he said to them, "These are my words that I spoke to you while I was still with you, that *everything written about me in the Law of Moses and the Prophets and the Psalms must be fulfilled.*" Then he opened their minds to understand the Scriptures, and said to them, "Thus it is written, that **the Christ should suffer** and **on the third day rise from the dead**." (Luke 24:44–46)

---

5. Likewise John Murray writes, "The reality of our sin and the reality of the wrath of God upon us for our sin do not come into our reckoning. And this is the reason why the gospel of justification is to such an extent a meaningless sound in the world and in the church of the twentieth century. We are not imbued with the profound sense of the reality of God, of his majesty and holiness. And sin, if reckoned with at all, is little more than misfortune or maladjustment." *Redemption Accomplished and Applied*, 123–24.

In the *italicized* text, Jesus explicitly states that *all of Scripture*, which at the time was generally the Old Testament, is about himself.[6] However, Jesus specifies what aspects of himself Scripture highlights. Rather than pointing to his miracles or teaching, he points to his **death** and **resurrection** (see the **bold** text). In other words, *all of Scripture* is about Jesus, especially his **death** and **resurrection**.[7] If our engagement with Scripture does not lead to a richer appreciation for the death and resurrection of Christ, then we are not in line with what Jesus plainly outlines here. In the words of Jesus, we are just like the "foolish ones" who are "slow of heart to believe all that the prophets have spoken" (Luke 24:25).

Relatedly, Scripture claims that the life of a Christian is equally about Christ—particularly his death and resurrection. As Paul writes, we are merely jars of clay who are meant to be broken so that the treasure of Christ can be manifest (2 Cor 4:7–12): "We are afflicted in every way . . . always carrying in the body the death of Jesus, so that the life of Jesus may also be manifested in our bodies" (2 Cor 4:8, 10). This treasure of Christ, however, is not his power or wisdom; instead, it is specifically his death and resurrection (2 Cor 4:10, 14): "Knowing that he who raised the Lord Jesus will raise us also with Jesus" (2 Cor 4:14). Manifesting the treasure of Christ through our broken lives is possible because those of us who are in Christ have been crucified with him (Gal 2:20). We no longer live, and instead the life of Christ reigns in our mortal bodies.

Therefore, *every* part of *both* Scripture and our lives is grounded, saturated, and culminating in Christ. The problem, however, is that the way we read life and live Scripture are often fragmented. We see Christ meaningfully and organically in certain areas of life or Scripture; but in other areas, we either do not see his relevance (i.e., not meaningful) or his relevance feels forced (i.e., not organic). We are accustomed to seeing Christ in certain parts of Scripture where the connection is obvious—for instance, specific events, narratives, prophecies, or "types" that are later explicitly identified as connected to Christ. As an unintended result, we red-letter our Bibles—that is, the way we mark the explicit words of Christ in the Gospels is similar to how we only see Christ in parts of the Bible

---

6. Although some do not interpret Luke 24:44 to say that *every* passage of the Old Testament is about Christ (e.g., Bovon, *Luke 3*), this claim is elsewhere made in other passages (e.g., John 5:39; 2 Cor 1:20).

7. The emphasis on the death and resurrection of Christ does not mean that other aspects of Jesus are not important. As we see later, his life of righteousness is essential. For a fuller treatment on this, see Crowe, *Perfect Life*.

Introduction

that have clear typological connections. All the Gospels, however, are Jesus's revelation; similarly, every part of Scripture finds its true purpose in him alone. Seeing Scripture in this way has profound implications for how we see our lives. Scripture is emphatically clear that our reality does not partially belong to Christ, as if we can red-letter certain aspects (e.g., going to church, when making significant decisions). Instead, every part of reality organically finds its true meaning in Christ alone.

Thankfully, God does not solely give us his word, but he gives an approach with interpretive principles to understand it as intended. In fact, God lays out these principles in the first three chapters of Scripture. Each of them is simple to understand but difficult to apply consistently with discipline. Without the Holy Spirit, it is indeed impossible (e.g., John 14:26; 1 Cor 2:10–16; Eph 1:17–19, 3:16–19). So this book seeks to foster a prayerful posture more than transmit information.

THE MAKEUP OF THE BOOK

When I have taught this approach in various venues—from church congregations of different age groups and denominations to academic classrooms—the results have been well beyond my expectations. However, the transformation for most takes time, with repeated application and reflection. Thus, recipients continually request the need for these principles to be available in a written format for further reflection and application, which is one of the purposes of this book.

This book touches upon many significant concepts and ideas that require more nuance and explanation than space can provide. So I have added notes to point readers to resources that have explored these more extensively. Instead, this book seeks to exude the tone of Scripture, which is more of a suspenseful story than an informative lecture.[8] Additionally, this book focuses more on providing guides and diagrams so that readers can apply the approach on their own. Lastly, as much as some of these concepts are interesting and important, this book's singular aim is to show how we can see Christ organically and meaningfully in every part of Scripture and life.

---

8. As Geerhardus Vos notes, "The Bible is not a dogmatic handbook but a historical book full of dramatic interest." *Biblical Theology*, 26.

THE OUTLINE OF THE BOOK

Chapter 1 reflects upon the way God introduces himself and humanity in the opening chapters of Scripture (Gen 1–3). From this reflection, we gather biblical principles that are the basis for the approach for understanding Scripture as intended.

Chapter 2 elaborates on the biblical principles and outlines the approach for understanding Scripture as intended. All of this is embedded in Gen 1–3 and developed further in other parts of Scripture. Since the first chunk of Scripture is written mostly in narrative, the chapter explains how to apply this approach for all narratives. One of the implications of this is that God is always the main character and everyone else—including Adam, Moses, and David—are merely side characters. The combination of chapters 1 and 2 demonstrates how Gen 1–3 foreshadows Christ as the True Adam.

Once it is shown that this approach and its interpretive principles are established by God's own word, the rest of the chapters demonstrate how this approach can be applied to select passages. As much as this approach can be applied to every part of Scripture, these passages are chosen because they cover much ground in the overall story of Scripture. Accordingly, chapter 3 fast-forwards to Exod 19–20 and 24. We explore key concepts such as the Mosaic covenant, law, and tabernacle through this approach. We are also introduced to another genre: biblical laws. This chapter therefore explains how this approach can be applied to biblical laws so that even in them we see the excellencies of Christ in a meaningful and organic way. If chapters 1 and 2 imply that Christ is the True Adam, then in chapter 3, he is the True Israel.

Chapter 4 presents another example of how to apply this approach by moving ahead to another major phase of biblical history: the monarchy. We again apply the approach to narratives involving David. One of the recurring themes surrounding David is the importance of genealogies. This chapter therefore shows how this approach can be applied to genealogies. When the dust settles, we behold Christ as the True David.

Through chapters 1–4, various New Testament passages are drawn, but their significance is not directly shown until chapter 5. Here we see more robustly how Christ is the True Adam, True Israel, and True David. All the glorious promises adumbrated in the Old Testament are dramatically fulfilled in Christ alone in the New Testament. The seeds of Christ that have been sown in the earlier chapters blossom here.

Introduction

Lastly, the conclusion provides reflections that reinforce our need *and* desire for Christ, which should foster prayerfulness and dependence on the Spirit. There is also an appendix that briefly introduces how this approach can be applied to the Writings or the wisdom literature and the Prophets of the Old Testament.

The hope of this book is that the approach and its examples can enhance all future engagements in God's word. This will not only enrich our understanding of Scripture but will have direct implications for how we see the gospel and ultimately all of reality. Indeed, the gospel enables us to live according to a basic truth that we consistently overlook and rarely apply: everything is thoroughly grounded, saturated, and culminating in Christ alone.[9]

QUESTIONS FOR REFLECTION AND PRAYER

a. Why should the death *and* resurrection of Christ be prominent in our lives and in our engagement with God's word?

b. In what ways can you relate with the struggle that your life and engagement in God's word do not orbit around Christ as much as they should?

c. Scripture makes it clear that without the Holy Spirit, it is impossible to understand God's word as intended (e.g., John 14:26; 1 Cor 2:10–16; Eph 1:17–19, 3:16–19). How can you be more prayerful in your engagement with God's word? Perhaps start by praying *before* your reading of Scripture (and asking the Spirit to help make your reading be prayerful) and pray *after* your reading of Scripture.

d. Before starting the next chapter, prayerfully read Gen 1–3 and make note of everything that you learn about God's character and promises.

---

9. So Graeme Goldsworthy writes, "The Bible makes a very radical idea inescapable: not only is the gospel the interpretive norm for the whole Bible, but there is an important sense in which Jesus Christ is the mediator of the meaning of everything that exists. In other words, *the gospel is the hermeneutical norm for the whole of reality*. All reality was created by Christ, through Christ and for Christ (Col. 1:15–16)." *Gospel-Centered Hermeneutics*, 63; emphasis original.

1

In the Beginning
Jesus Christ as the True Adam (Gen 1–3)

People love stories. No matter where you are in the world or when you exist in history, everyone gravitates not only around compelling stories but effective story tellers. One of the most frustrating aspects of hearing a great story is when someone interrupts that story. Perhaps someone incessantly interjects with irrelevant questions or somehow makes the story about something entirely different—maybe even him or herself.

That the most common genre of Scripture is a story (or to be more technical, "narrative") is a well-known fact. But have we considered what this says about who God is? He is full of personality, life, love, wisdom, and every other virtue that we can imagine. Additionally, have we considered how we might hijack his stories? Every part of Scripture is ultimately about himself—his character and promises, all of which culminate in Jesus Christ. Yet often we make these narratives about ourselves or other secondary concerns.

This chapter interprets Gen 1–3 so that we glean biblical principles that recur not only in the rest of Scripture but in our everyday lives. In other words, these biblical principles serve as a template for how to live Scripture and read life. As captivating as Gen 1–3 is as a story, it is even more instructive as a guide. After gleaning these biblical principles, the next chapter (chapter 2) outlines the approach to Scripture and life based on these principles. The reason why we begin with Gen 1–3 rather than the approach is to emphasize that the approach is derived from Scripture and

GENESIS 1:1—2:3: THE GOD WHO CREATES

Genesis 1:1-2: The God Who Is Independent

First impressions are the most lasting ones. The way God introduces himself in Scripture is supposed to color the way we perceive him in every other biblical passage and in life. The opening verses imply that prior to creation, there was nothing:[1]

> In the beginning, God created the heavens and the earth. The earth was without form and void, and darkness was over the face of the deep. And the Spirit of God was hovering over the face of the waters. (Gen 1:1-2)

This point is reinforced later in New Testament passages, such as John 1:3 ("All things were made through him, and without him was not any thing made that was made") and Col 1:16 ("For by him all things were created, in heaven and on earth, visible and invisible, whether thrones or dominions or rulers or authorities—all things were created through him and for him").

The rest of Gen 1-2 explains how God creates. But before we reflect upon this, we must first acknowledge that God introduces himself as *the* CREATOR. Of course, God could have introduced himself as a father, master, judge, or many other roles. One of the fundamental reasons why he introduces himself as the CREATOR is that he is independent from his creation.[2] As much as the details of him creating emphasize his intimacy and relationality, which we explore below, the fact that he is the sole CREATOR and all of creation finds its existence upon him stresses how unique he is. This is the reason why God later designates himself as "I AM WHO I AM" (Exod 3:14). When God commissions Moses to deliver the people of Israel out of slavery from Egypt, Moses asks what name of God he should use when trying to convince others. God could have used the name earlier in

---

[1]. It has been debated whether Gen 1-2 raises and answers the question of God creating everything out of nothing. What is clear is that other parts of Scripture provide an answer (e.g., Pss 33:6, 148:5; John 1:3; Col 1:16; etc.): everything has been created out of nothing by God. See, e.g., Arnold, *Genesis*, 35-36. For a more detailed interpretation on Gen 1-3 that reflects upon modern concerns, see Poythress, *Interpreting Eden*.

[2]. This is also referred to as the "aseity" of God.

the conversation that is more common, "the God of Abraham, the God of Isaac, and the God of Jacob" (Exod 3:6; cf. 3:15), but for the specific purpose of conveying God's essence, he gives a different name: "I AM WHO I AM. . . . Say this to the people of Israel: 'I AM has sent me to you'" (Exod 3:14).[3]

The CREATOR and I AM are fitting names because they remind us of something that we consistently overlook: God is independent. The concept of a king, for instance, is not as adequate to describe who God is because a king ultimately needs a kingdom and subjects. The CREATOR, however, is not dependent on anything. There is no need or lack in him. Whatever he desires, he can simply create. Hence, the most essential way that God describes himself is in reference to himself: I AM WHO I AM. God is simply outside of anything that we can conceptualize.

If the independence of God is part of his self-introduction, then it should shape the way we understand him, his word, and all of creation.[4] For instance, all things are absolutely dependent on God for *everything*—not only for their purpose but even their *existence* (John 1:3, Heb 1:3). Everything was not only created *by* and *through* God but *for* him (Col 1:16). This means that all of reality, including the moral of every story and the point of every narrative, is ultimately about God. As such, God's word is fundamentally about himself. He alone is the main character of every story. Although side characters like Adam, Abraham, Moses, and others are important, God does not need them. They are merely windows of God's gracious revelation of himself.[5] In the next chapter, we unpack this more through the concept of the CREATOR-*creature Distinction*.

---

3. The significance of this designation cannot be fully explored here. See Carol L. Meyers's commentary that shows its connection to the Tetragrammaton and how it could not even be pronounced out of reverence for God (Meyers, *Exodus*, 57–59).

4. This becomes especially apparent when understanding the ancient Near Eastern context as John H. Walton points out (*Lost World of Genesis One*, 142–43). From a systematic-theological perspective, Bavinck writes, "The first thing Scripture teaches us concerning God is that he has a free, independent existence and life of his own that is distinct from all creatures. . . . God is independent in everything; in his existence, in his perfections, in his decrees, and in his works." *Reformed Dogmatics*, 2:150, 153.

5. Abraham Kuyper similarly writes, "In his entire Theology, the Theologian must stand in the presence of God as his God, and as soon as for a single instant he looks away from the living God, in order to engage himself with an idea about God over which he will sit as judge, he is lost in phraseology, because the object of his knowledge has already vanished from his view." *Encyclopedia of Sacred Theology*, 252.

IN THE BEGINNING

Genesis 1:3–25: The God Who Is Methodical, Joyful, and Artistic

When we imagine someone who is independent, we might perceive that person to be aloof. Aloofness, however, is not how God reveals himself. These verses are replete with details that convey God being full of life and personality. We sadly overlook these important aspects of God because we often hijack this passage by fixating on questions that are alien to the text (e.g., How old is earth? Does evolutionary theory render this account primitive?). If we apply the simple principle that all of reality is fundamentally about God, what might we learn about him in this creation account? Though the independent CREATOR has no need for anything, out of the fullness of love, he creates everything methodically, joyfully, and artistically for the benefit of humanity.

God methodically creates everything with remarkable symmetry. The first three days, God is separating; the final three days, God is populating the very things that he separated:

Separation	Population
1. Light versus darkness (Gen 1:1–5)	4. Greater and lesser lights (1:14–19)
2. Heavenly versus earthly realms (1:6–8)	5. Sea creatures and birds (1:20–25)
3. Water versus land (1:9–13)	6. Land creatures and humanity (1:26–31)

As methodical as God is, he is also joyful. After each day of creation, he goes out of his way to remark that his work is "good" and ensures that this remark is recorded in his word (Gen 1:4, 10, 12, 18, 21, 25, 31)! The only day on which he does not make any comment is day two, which is when he separates the heavenly realm from the earthly (Gen 1:6–8)—a point that I explain later in the book.[6]

Another pattern that emerges is the recurring phrase "according to its kind" (Gen 1:11, 12 [x2], 21 [x2], 24 [x2], 25 [x3]). This phrase occurs a total of ten times! When God creates the plants, sea creatures, birds, and land creatures, he does not create just enough to ensure that the ecosystem can be maintained. Rather, his creation brims with diversity and creativity. The

---

6. There are different interpretations for day two (e.g., Poythress, *Interpreting Eden*, 171–86). But as we see later in chapters 3 and 5, the connection between Exod 24:9–11, Ezek 1:22–28, and Rev 21 is one of the many reasons why I interpret it as a separation between the heavenly and earthly realms. For a recent commentary on day two, see Hendel, *Genesis 1–11*, 116–20.

beauty of creation that has mesmerized botanists and zoologists is merely a symptom of the artistry of God.

Part of the reason why God creates so methodically, joyfully, and artistically is that this is simply who he is intrinsically. In his excellence, all his works are excellent by any measure. However, the next passage reveals another reason for why God's creation is so methodical, joyful, and artistic: his love for humanity.

Genesis 1:26—2:3: The God Who Loves

Genesis 1 has a certain rhythm. With each passing day, a pleasant tension builds. The rhythm is elegantly suspended on the second half of the sixth day when the CREATOR creates humanity (Gen 1:26-31):

1. While God speaks everything into existence on each day, nowhere does he refer to himself to make something: for example, "Let there be light" versus "Let us make man in our image" (Gen 1:3, 26).

2. As "good" as all of his creation has been thus far, nothing has been created in his own image (Gen 1:26).

3. As methodical, joyful, and artistic as God's creation is, all of it is generously entrusted to humanity (Gen 1:26, 28-30).

4. Everything else God created is "good," but only humanity is "very good" (Gen 1:31).

While the ultimate purpose of God's creation is to glorify himself (Col 1:16), the details above reveal that this is connected to God's love for humanity. God creates everything in such a way to express his love for humanity. Just like how mothers instinctively know to nest—diligently preparing an environment that enables their babies to flourish—the CREATOR lovingly orders reality so that humanity can thrive. This is why in the second version of the creation account (Gen 2:4-24), the dominating focus is how God creates humanity, his magnum opus.

The climax of the creation account, however, is not until the seventh day (Gen 2:1-3). On this day, God rests and portrays himself as a worker. This, however, raises a question: Why would the independent CREATOR "need" rest? The details revealed in Gen 1 hardly suggest arduous work. God, in his omnipotence, simply spoke all of reality into existence. As the skilled storyteller, God does not answer this question until later. At that point, we learn that the seventh day is the Sabbath. God takes the Sabbath very seriously because it is fundamentally a day on which his people can be reminded of his character and promises, which includes him creating everything lovingly for the benefit of humanity. Much like how parents bond with their children over a shared activity, the CREATOR has instituted the Sabbath so that intimacy can be forged repeatedly with his creatures.

The moral of this set of verses, then, is not that humanity is lovable. The rest of Scripture makes this increasingly clear. Instead, the point of these details is to reveal something about the main character: God is loving. One of the tragedies of God's revelation, including this one, is that we twist the emphasis to be on humanity rather than God. This then devolves into magnifying the potential goodness of people rather than God's long-suffering and undeserving love. We redirect this truth that is intended to feature God by inserting ourselves as the main character.

GENESIS 2:4–25: THE GOD WHO PROVIDES

The second version of the creation account discloses more details regarding how God creates and relates with humanity. We cannot pay attention to every detail, so we only reflect upon the way God provides humanity with food, an environment, a purpose, partnership, and laws.

The God Who Provides Food

The story repeatedly hints at the quality of food that God provides humanity since this is an important part of the plot. In Gen 1, the vast array of plants that God creates "according to their own kinds" (1:11, 12) is all made available for humanity to enjoy. This provision is already repeated twice in the first version of the creation account: "I have given you every plant yielding seed that is on the face of all the earth, and every tree with seed in its fruit. You shall have them for food" (Gen 1:29) and "I have given every green plant for food" (Gen 1:30). Now in this second version, we learn that God creates for humanity "every tree that is pleasant to the sight and good for food" (Gen 2:9). In other words, God's provision is not only abundant and diverse, but it is both sumptuous and nutritious. Seeing it is salivating; consuming it is nourishing. Like all good stories, these seemingly unimportant details will be significant.

The God Who Provides the Ideal Environment

The chapter then describes the environment of the garden of Eden that might seem random (Gen 2:10–14). When we are disciplined in seeing God as the main character, such information makes sense. The garden is nurtured by four rivers and contains the choice materials of gold and onyx.[7] These details further cement the idea that God has nested the ideal setting for humanity to flourish.

The God Who Provides a Glorious Purpose

God also provides a sense of purpose for the man: "The LORD God took the man and put him in the garden of Eden to work it and keep it" (Gen 2:15). At face value, this purpose might seem menial or cumbersome. But earlier, God reveals himself as a worker (Gen 2:1–3). Thus, God assigns humanity a noble task, not merely to solve the problem of working the ground (Gen 2:5) but so that the CREATOR and creature can enjoy the shared experience of work, adding another way of nurturing their relationship. As we will soon see, work does become laborious since it is tarnished by sin. Prior to sin, however, work is portrayed as a dignified activity since God portrays himself as a worker wherein he executed his work methodically, joyfully, and artistically.

Additionally, the task that God has given the man is lofty. The verbs, "to work it and keep it" (Gen 2:15), are later used to describe the role of priests (e.g., Num 3:7–8, 18:5–6).[8] Priests fulfill an office that is precious to God. God grants the priests the closest access to his presence. From this sacred role, priests become an expression of God's holiness as well as his mercy since they facilitate fellowship between the common people and God. Thus, God gave the man a role so that he can have access to God's presence, share in God's holiness, and help others enjoy God's intimacy.

---

7. Hence, water, gold, and onyx appear in the tabernacle, temple, and the new creation (e.g., Exod 25:7, 11, 17, 31; 30:17–21; 1 Kgs 6:21–22, 7:23–39; 1 Chr 29:2; Rev 21:18, 20–21; 22:1–2).

8. From the Hebrew ʿavad and *shamar*.

The God Who Provides Partnership

God also provides the man with a "helper fit for him" (Gen 2:18). Since God commissions humanity to "be fruitful and multiply and fill the earth" (Gen 1:28), procreation is needed. Up until now, the man does not have suitable a partner with whom he can procreate. God is not only the one who provides, but he does so with romance. God has Adam review and name every single animal, only to be left with the dissatisfying emptiness that "for Adam there was not found a helper fit for him" (Gen 2:19–20). At this point God causes Adam to fall into a "deep sleep," creates the woman out of Adam's own flesh to convey intimacy, and brings her to Adam so that she is the first thing he sees when he awakes (Gen 2:21–22)! This sequence of events orchestrated by God conveys the same kind of methodical, joyful, and artistic manner that we saw earlier. Adam's reaction explodes with elation as he exclaims the first expression of human poetry, compelling him to "hold fast to his wife" so that they can experience the bliss of becoming "one flesh" without any shame (Gen 2:23–25).

The God Who Provides Laws

Lastly, God issues a few commands or laws. For the purposes of this chapter, we look at only two of them:

1. Humanity to "subdue it [the earth] and have dominion over the fish of the sea and over the birds of the heavens and over every living thing that moves on the earth" (Gen 1:28b).
2. "You may surely eat of every tree of the garden, but of the tree of the knowledge of good and evil you shall not eat, for in the day that you eat of it you shall surely die" (Gen 2:16–17).

When we think of laws, we typically feel a sense of burden. Laws have the reputation of being impersonal or insensitive to specific situations. So we often think of laws as arbitrary, and we certainly do not regard laws as an expression of love. Sometimes we even perceive lawgivers as authoritarian with ulterior motives.

Before we examine these two laws, we must be reminded of the simple fact that is difficult to apply consistently: God is the independent CREATOR. He does not need these laws, nor does he need us to follow them. His laws are not only for our benefit, but they primarily reveal something about his own character and promises. When we apply these truths to laws, we become overwhelmed, not with a sense of burden that we must mindlessly obey but with a profound appreciation for his character and promises.[9]

The first law is to subdue the earth and have dominion over all the animals. This is less a law or burden and more a privilege and invitation—which is the case for all of God's laws. In this law, humanity is bestowed with the highest role. After creating everything methodically, joyfully, and artistically, God generously commits all his glorious creation to humanity. Moreover, God does not leave humanity to figure this out on their own. Instead, God lovingly brings every animal to the man so that the man can name every animal. As we know, and especially in the ancient Near Eastern context of the Old Testament, naming something conveys one's authority. In short, what we learn from this simple law is that God is full of authority, but he wants to share that authority with humanity. If Sabbath and work are the shared activities that foster fellowship between the independent CREATOR and his dependent creatures, then having dominion is now added for that same purpose. As humanity relates with God and enjoys his gentle reign over their lives, humanity can then exert that over the rest of creation. In essence, this law to subdue and have dominion is more of an invitation for humanity to appreciate God's loving rule over them and to live according to the privileged role given by God.

The second law of not eating from the tree of the knowledge of good and evil is almost always misunderstood. Instead of considering what this law says about God's character and promises, we typically fall into philosophical debates about what this tree represents. Did humanity not know good or evil prior to eating the tree? And should not God know better? Surely if you tell someone not to do something, then that person is even more tempted to do that exact thing!

In order to understand this law as intended, we must be disciplined to consider first what it says about God's character and promises. Recognizing all the clues that have been mentioned above is a good starting point: God has extravagantly provided humanity with countless plants that are all pleasing to the sight and good for food (Gen 1:11–12, 29–30; 2:9). In a way, God has given humanity a perpetual buffet, except every item in this buffet is of the utmost quality! Thus, every time humanity eats from one of

---

9. To be clear, God's law does require obedience, as Crowe has recently demonstrated (*Perfect Life*, 35–84). The point that I am making is that obedience is designed to flow from a trust in who God is. For more on this, see chapter 2.

these trees *or* does not eat from the tree of the knowledge of good and evil, humanity should be reminded of God's character and promises—not the dos and don'ts of the law. If the first law is a continual reminder to humanity that God is generously sharing his authority, then the second law is a continual reminder that God is lavishly providing. I will provide a more systematic way of interpreting all the biblical laws as intended in chapter 3.

At the same time, the clarity of this prohibition with the explicit consequence of death ("you shall surely die") is not because God is stern. Instead, the clarity is to equip Adam so that he can detect lies that might confuse God's revelation. Thus, the clarity is not to be misunderstood as strictness but as love. This frequently misunderstood detail will also become significant in the story.[10]

GENESIS 3:1–6: HUMANITY'S RESPONSE

If God has meticulously provided humanity everything to flourish, including laws that are perpetual reminders of his character and promises, then surely humanity will respond with trust, obedience, and adoration. There is, sadly, a plot twist. Adam and Eve reject God's provisions, which is the first instance of sin. The way this rebellion develops offers an incisive perspective on the essence of sin and why it is so tempting. So although there are many profound truths that can be extracted from this passage, we focus only on what it reveals about sin. In short, the essence of sin is a distrust of God by distorting, suppressing, and/or rejecting his character or promises.

Genesis 3:1–3: Humanity Distorts God's Character or Promises

Genesis 3 begins by describing that "the serpent was more crafty than any other beast of the field that the Lord God had made" (Gen 3:1). There are at least two relevant details revealed. First is that the serpent is indeed the craftiest of all the beasts. Anyone who interacts with the serpent should therefore be careful. Second, although the serpent is crafty, it is still a "beast

---

10. Parents, teachers, and similar roles know the wisdom behind explicit instructions and consequences. For instance, children and students might recognize the wisdom behind certain values, but unless there are specific instructions and consequences clearly communicated, it is extremely difficult for children and students to live according to such values. Similarly, God communicates concrete instructions and consequences for our sake.

of the field that the LORD God had made." This mirrors an earlier phrase, "The LORD God formed every beast of the field" (Gen 2:19). The context of this earlier phrase is that God presents to Adam every animal. We saw earlier that naming is an assertion of one's dominion. Moreover, because Adam saw every animal, he knew the individual characteristics of each one. So God equipped Adam to be fully knowledgeable of the craftiness of the serpent and have authority over it, as well as a law that is clear and explicit so that Adam would not be confused. We shortly see how Adam neglects these privileges and responsibilities, leaving his wife vulnerable while defying his loving CREATOR.

The serpent addresses the woman with a seemingly innocent question about God's law (Gen 3:1). When comparing the serpent's question with the original command, the motivation becomes clear:

Gen 2:16b–17	Gen 3:1b
You may surely eat of **every tree of the garden**, but of the tree of the knowledge of good and evil *you shall not eat*, for in the day that you eat of it you shall surely die.	Did God actually say, "*You shall not eat* of **any tree in the garden?**"

The serpent is using the same words of God's command but jumbling them to create a contrary emphasis and meaning:

1. God's command begins with a *privilege*, "*You may surely eat*," but the serpent begins the quotation with a *restriction*, "*You shall not eat.*"
2. God's command is a reminder that "**every tree of the garden**" has been provided as food; the serpent implies that not a single tree in the garden can be eaten ("**any tree in the garden**").
3. There is *only one singular* tree that *cannot* be eaten, while the serpent insinuates that there is *no singular* tree that *can* be eaten.

In short, the serpent is distorting God's command in subtle ways so that the command does not appear to be a gracious reminder of God's provision, but one that is stringent.

Eve's initial reply appears like she sees through this tactic, "We may eat of the fruit of the trees in the garden" (Gen 3:2), but ultimately she does not recognize this distortion. In fact, she plays into it by adding "neither shall you touch it, lest you die" (Gen 3:3). Eve's addition indicates the way she perceives the law and ultimately God's character and promises. Rather than seeing this law as a perpetual reminder of God's generosity, this addition implies that both God and his word are harsh.

Genesis 3:4–5: Humanity Suppresses God's Character or Promises

Now that Adam and Eve have distorted God's law and character, the serpent increases the lie even further. This becomes clear when we compare the serpent's interpretation of the law with the original:

Gen 2:16b–17	Gen 3:4
You may surely eat of every tree of the garden, but of the tree of the knowledge of good and evil you shall not eat, for in the day that you eat of it *you shall surely die*.	But the serpent said to the woman, "*You will not surely die.*"

If the serpent was subtly challenging God's word earlier, he is now directly defying it. God plainly says, "You shall surely die," while the serpent says, "You will not surely die." There are many mixed messages signalled with this attack on God's word. Before, the serpent implies that God is severe; now, the serpent implies that he is deceitful or weak. Is God a liar? Is he not capable of fulfilling his own word?

The serpent offers an explanation that impugns God's character—which is at the core of sin. God is not trustworthy: "For God knows that when you eat of it your eyes will be opened, and you will be like God, knowing good and evil" (Gen 3:5). In other words, God is withholding goodness from you. He is not after your best interests. Eve (and Adam) do not correct the serpent this time. They remain silent. They have not only fallen prey to distorting God's law and his character, but they are now suppressing all that they have known and experienced about God. God has been relational and intimate with Adam and Eve, lovingly sharing his presence with them (Gen 3:8). They are bombarded with evidence of God's care and power every time they eat other plants and interact with other creatures. All of reality has been curated by God for them to be unceasingly confronted with his love and majesty. Here we see why God was so clear and explicit with the prohibition, so that Adam (and Eve) could recognize that the deceit is in the serpent instead of in God. However, in their mental measuring scales, they are placing greater weight on the claims of the serpent—a creature over which they have dominion!—rather than in the word of God—the independent CREATOR whose grace and righteousness emanate in every aspect of reality.

Genesis 3:6: Humanity Rejects God's Character or Promises

Once Adam and Eve distort and suppress God's character and promises, their rejection of God is imminent. The irony is that some of the aspects of the fruit that attract the woman are the very ones that are present in every other plant that has been freely given by God:

Gen 2:9a	Gen 3:6a
And out of the ground the LORD God made to spring up every tree that is **pleasant to the sight** and *good for food*.	So when the woman saw that the tree was *good for food*, and that it was a **delight to the eyes** ...

Eve seeks the forbidden fruit because it was "*good for food*" and a "**delight to the eyes**," when every other fruit that God provided was "*good for food*" and "**pleasant to the sight**." As Paul later explains in the New Testament, when we distort and suppress God's character and promises, our thinking becomes deranged even if we feel like we are being reasonable at that time or celebrated by others (since they too are deranged!) (Rom 1:18–32).[11] Thus, biting the very hand that feeds us rarely feels foolish; often it feels right. In the next chapter, we explore further into this *Problem of Sin*.

Adam (who was present the whole time!) and Eve finally reject God's laws (Gen 3:6). Eating the fruit is not rejecting just one law (Gen 2:16–17) but also the law to have dominion over the creatures (Gen 1:28, 2:19–20). Moreover, it is fundamentally a spurning of God's character and promises. Adam and Eve are essentially snubbing their nose to all the gracious provisions that we observed. They are choosing to place their trust in fellow creatures who owe their very existence to the independent CREATOR, while turning their backs on the independent CREATOR by whom and for whom all things exist. As a result of this treacherous and foolish rebellion, humanity has severed themselves from the only source of goodness.

---

11. The word "deranged" has been inspired by Vos's trenchant description of sin: "Sin has deranged the original relation between God and man. It has produced a separation where previously perfect communion prevailed. From the nature of the case every step towards rectifying this abnormality must spring from God's sovereign initiative. This particular aspect, therefore, of the indispensableness of revelation stands or falls with the recognition of the fact of sin." *Biblical Theology*, 12.

In the Beginning

GENESIS 3:7–24: THE GOD WHO WITHHOLDS WRATH AND PROMISES SALVATION

Genesis 3:7–24 → Old Testament → Christ

The consequence of Adam and Eve's sin is death as God warned explicitly (Gen 2:17). For the purposes of this book, it suffices to regard this as a spiritual death.[12] This is expressed through the exile from the garden of Eden, which is sealed by the guarding cherubim at the east (Gen 3:22–24)—a detail that we will revisit.

Later Scripture explains that because Adam had dominion over all of creation, his sin has a cascading effect that tarnishes every aspect of creation (e.g., Rom 5:12–21, 8:19–23). One of the implications of this is that every human is spiritually dead and born with a sinful nature. Theologians refer to this role of Adam as federal headship.[13] The unique role and the substantial consequences of Adam set the context for Jesus's role as the True Adam.

Although the promises of Christ are not explicitly clear until later in Scripture, they are adumbrated in how God responds to Adam and Eve's rebellion. Imagine the scene: Adam and Eve plainly defy God's laws. As God is confronting the guilty parties, they know full well that the sentence is death (Gen 2:17). Yet as they are hearing the consequences of their rebellion, God is indirectly making promises(!):[14]

Guilty Party	Consequence of Sin	Promise of Life
The serpent	"I will put enmity between you and the woman, and between your offspring and her offspring" (Gen 3:15).	The woman will have *offspring*, implying that she and Adam will live!
The woman	"I will surely multiply your pain in childbearing; in pain you shall bring forth children" (Gen 3:16).	The woman has *the ability to bear children*, implying that she and Adam will live!
Adam	"By the sweat of your face you shall eat bread" (Gen 3:19).	Adam will *work*, implying that he will live!

12. Waltke, *Genesis*, 86–87.

13. For more, see Crowe, *Last Adam*.

14. John Goldingay also recognizes the suspense: "The surprise lies in the fact that death does not follow. Yet there is also something surprising about a holy book that begins with a command that is immediately disobeyed and a God who fails to carry out a threat." *Genesis*, 62. Though I would not imply that God is not faithful to his word.

So despite Adam and Eve's sin in the face of the CREATOR's blessings, God nonetheless responds by making promises. Just like the gospel of Christ, in the face of deserving death and God's punishment, God instead extends further mercy. Moreover, the implications of these promises are immense. It takes the rest of Scripture to unpack these implications. Indeed, these promises are akin to an outline for how the plot of Scripture thickens.

(1) The first provision is a promise of redemption (Gen 3:15). Eventually one of the offsprings of Eve will be the one who will vindicate humanity by destroying the serpent.

(2) Although the consequence of Adam and Eve's rebellion is death, God still preserves the ability for Eve to bear children (Gen 3:16), and Eve is later named by Adam as the mother of all living (Gen 3:20).[15]

(3) In order for fellowship to be maintained between the holy CREATOR and the creatures who are now sinful, some kind of covering of shame, which involves the killing of animals, is procured (Gen 3:21).

(4) God does not destroy the tree of life or the garden of Eden but maintains them, implying that these are reserved for a future purpose (Gen 3:22–24).

These are all seeds of salvation, each of which sprout and grow dynamically in the Old Testament until they are finally fulfilled in Christ. So all of Scripture is interconnected, which can be understood with the concept of the *Organism of Scripture*.[16] In the next chapter, we explore this concept more fully, but for now it suffices to recognize that the latter half of Gen 3 is a rough outline of the rest of Scripture:

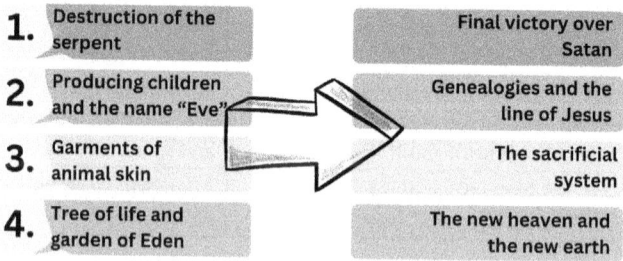

1. Destruction of the serpent → Final victory over Satan
2. Producing children and the name "Eve" → Genealogies and the line of Jesus
3. Garments of animal skin → The sacrificial system
4. Tree of life and garden of Eden → The new heaven and the new earth

---

15. Similarly, Hendel, *Genesis 1–11*, 191.

16. Scripture as organism can be seen as early as Kuyper and Bavinck (e.g., Brock and Sutanto, *Neo-Calvinism*, 98–132). For the exact phrase, see Bavinck, *Reformed Dogmatics*, 1:16. My development of it is influenced by Vos, *Biblical Theology*, 11–27.

Christ → Death and Resurrection

If these provisions are ultimately fulfilled by Christ, how exactly does he fulfill them? Similarly, if all of Scripture is about Jesus, what aspects of Jesus are central? There are so many glorious aspects of Jesus, so it is easy to get lost in his love, wisdom, or his power. As we saw in the introduction, Jesus explains that Scripture does not point to generic things about himself. Instead, he points to two specific things: his death and resurrection (Luke 24:44–46). This is why Paul has "decided to know nothing among you except Jesus Christ and him crucified" (1 Cor 2:2; see also 1 Cor 1:23, Gal 6:14). Later in this same epistle, Paul elaborates further: "For I delivered to you as of first importance what I also received: that Christ died for our sins in accordance with the Scriptures, that he was buried, that he was raised on the third day in accordance with the Scriptures" (1 Cor 15:3–4). With the repetition of the phrase "accordance with the Scriptures," we can summarize the entire Bible by understanding the Old Testament as anticipating the death and resurrection of Christ, while the New Testament is unpacking the implications of the death and resurrection of Christ:[17]

Since the storyteller makes it clear that all the stories of Scripture are about himself, specifically his death and resurrection, how often are we hijacking these stories and making them about something else?[18] In essence, this is precisely what happened in Gen 3 where the serpent twists God's laws into something that they do not intend. The next chapter outlines an approach toward understanding Scripture based on the biblical principles gleaned in this chapter so that we can see the rest of Scripture as intended. As a result, we will organically and meaningfully appreciate the death and resurrection of Christ throughout Scripture and ultimately in our everyday life.

---

17. As Bavinck writes, "Whereas in the Old Testament everything led up to Christ, in the New Testament everything is derived from Him. Christ is the turning point of times." *Our Reasonable Faith*, 94.

18. Likewise, Vern S. Poythress asserts that the redemption by Christ "is *the* one central story." *In the Beginning*, 206; emphasis original.

QUESTIONS FOR REFLECTION AND PRAYER

a. One of the important implications of this book is that God is the main character and we are the side characters.

  1. How does this simple principle help you understand Gen 1–3 better? For instance, what aspects of God's character and promises revealed in these chapters do you find surprising or praiseworthy?

  2. In what ways do you find God being the main character of Scripture and your life refreshing? In what ways do you resist this?

b. The Problem of Sin implies that the ultimate problem is that we distrust God by distorting, suppressing, and/or rejecting God's character or promises. Like Adam and Eve, we rarely recognize how absurd this is at the time. How might this understanding of sin be helpful for you as you live Scripture and read life?

c. In the face of judgment, God offers more promises and provisions for Adam and Eve—all of which are in Christ. How does God's response to Adam and Eve help you appreciate your own experience with God's unexpected and undeserving mercy?

d. Before reading the next chapter, how would you explain why are *both* the death and resurrection necessary?

2

Defining the Approach

CREATOR-Creature Distinction, the Problem of Sin, and the Organism of Scripture

GENESIS 1–3 IS SUCH an immersive story that it is easy to overlook some of its key biblical principles. These principles enable us to understand the rest of Scripture as intended. It is from these biblical principles that this chapter outlines an approach that is meant to be applied whenever we read Scripture. As a result, we will not only see Christ more meaningfully and organically throughout Scripture but also throughout our everyday life.

The three biblical principles of this approach are: (1) the CREATOR-creature Distinction, (2) the Problem of Sin, and (3) the Organism of Scripture. In short, the CREATOR-creature Distinction reminds us of the centrality of God and our utter dependence upon him; the Problem of Sin is humanity's refusal to see God for who he is; and the Organism of Scripture shows that all of Scripture is interconnected with its ultimate aim in Jesus Christ, who alone enables us to relate to God rightly.[1]

As basic as these individual principles are, it is important to see them in this sequence because this is how Scripture introduces them. Not consistently recognizing the CREATOR-creature Distinction will lead to a superficial grasp on the Problem of Sin, which will then lead to an artificial

---

1. These three are some of the most important concepts in the introduction to Vos's biblical theology (*Biblical Theology*, 11–27).

appreciation for the death and resurrection of Christ (the Organism of Scripture). Likewise, our appreciation for the death and resurrection of Christ (the Organism of Scripture) can only go as far as our grasp on the Problem of Sin; and our recognition of the Problem of Sin can only go as far as our recognition of the independence, sovereignty, righteousness, and holiness of God (CREATOR-creature Distinction).[2]

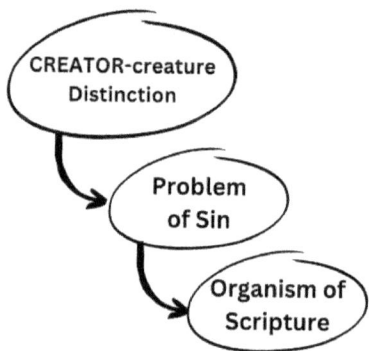

THE CREATOR-CREATURE DISTINCTION

In the previous chapter, we saw from Gen 1:1–2:24 that God introduces himself as the independent CREATOR. However, his independence does not make him impersonal. In fact, he creates all of reality methodically, joyfully, and artistically—all out of love for humanity. His love for humanity is further expressed in how he endows them with appetizing and nutritious food, an ideal environment to flourish, a glorious purpose, intimate partnership, and laws to remind them of his character and promises. All these details are examples of how God regularly interacts with his people throughout Scripture and even today. These can be summarized as God *revealing, condescending,* and *"covenanting"* (i.e., establishing a covenantal relationship) with his people. When we understand these fundamental ways that the CREATOR interacts with his creation, we see that the only proper response is to trust, obey, and adore.[3]

---

2. Note, however, that there are passages that present these principles in a different order, but the logical flow of it is always in this sequence.

3. This diagram is influenced by Cornelius Van Til's famous diagram (though I am adjusting it). I do not believe his diagram has ever been published, so for background, see Muether, *Cornelius Van Til*, 116; and Watkin, *Biblical Critical Theory*, 55–58. See also the resources at https://reformedforum.org/.

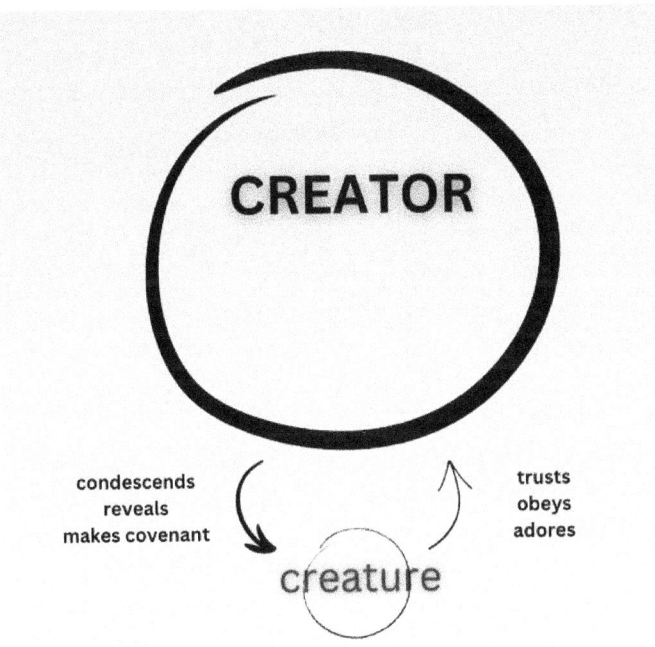

The God Who Condescends

Since God is the independent CREATOR, any interaction that he offers to his creation is one of condescension. Admittedly, condescending might have negative connotations. It would be quite off-putting if your friend agrees to your request to share a meal by saying, "Sure, I am willing to condescend to you!" However, in the context of the independent CREATOR being the source of all life, love, and joy, his willingness to stoop down to the level of his creation is an expression of generosity. Nothing intrinsically deserves God's attention since he simply has no need; moreover, everything is utterly dependent upon God for its meaning and existence. Thus, the sheer fact that he is aware and actually interacts with anything is a voluntary act of love. God is constantly accommodating to the level of inferior beings. In every passage of Scripture, we must be disciplined to think of God as the main character and that his mere consideration for others is one of condescending benevolence.[4]

---

4. The oft-cited quotation—albeit addressing a different issue—is relevant here: "For who even of slight intelligence does not understand that, as nurses commonly do with

The God Who Reveals

God not only graciously condescends, but he also reveals. In his independence, God is not obligated to reveal anything to humanity, nor does he benefit from it. Nevertheless he freely reveals his character and promises. If our favorite celebrity were to do the same for us, how thankful would we be?[5] Yet when God discloses such precious truths, we often take it for granted. We might dismiss God's revelation as inconvenient or irrelevant. Instead, the proper response is gratitude for gifting us with a glorious vantage point into who he is. All the virtues and values after which our souls long are bound within his character and promises—some of which God liberally shares with us.

Some might retort that they never heard God reveal anything. But Scripture repeatedly makes clear that all of creation is a declaration of his revelation. David confesses that "the heavens declare the glory of God, and the sky above proclaims his handiwork. Day to day pours out speech, and night to night reveals knowledge" (Ps 19:1–2). Paul explains that "God has shown . . . his invisible attributes, namely, his eternal power and divine nature, . . . ever since the creation of the world" (Rom 1:19–20). Thus, all of reality, including our consciousness, is a testimony of God revealing to his creation his character and promises. The question is not when is God speaking, but when is he *not* speaking?[6]

The God Who "Covenants"

Despite his independence, God willingly establishes a covenantal relationship with humanity. Covenants are intentional relationships based on shared experience that have stipulated expectations, promises, and

---

infants, God is wont in a measure to 'lisp' in speaking to us? Thus such forms of speaking do not so much express clearly what God is like as accommodate the knowledge of him to our slight capacity. To do this he must descend far beneath his loftiness." Calvin, *Institutes*, 1.13.1.

5. Kuyper's quote helps us not to take this simple fact for granted: "[The Theologian] *cannot* investigate God. There is nothing to analyze. There are no phenomena from which to draw conclusions. Only when that wondrous God will speak, can he listen. And thus the Theologian is absolutely *dependent* upon the pleasure of God, either to impart or not to impart knowledge of Himself." *Encyclopedia of Sacred Theology*, 251; italics original.

6. So Bavinck writes, "Because the universe is God's creation, it is also his revelation and self-manifestation. There is not an atom of the world that does not reflect his deity." *Reformed Dogmatics*, 2:109.

consequences. In the ancient Near East, covenants favor the more powerful party (e.g., a stronger king initiates a covenant with a weaker king who has been conquered).[7] But the covenantal relationship that God establishes with humanity is profoundly unusual. God's covenants are purely magnanimous. Instead of favoring the stronger party, they unexpectedly favor the weaker party. There is nothing for God to benefit from in his relationship with humanity because he is independent; there is everything for us to gain since he alone is the source of goodness. That God actually has expectations for how humans ought to relate to him and issues promises for the benefit of humans are once again astonishing instances of his munificence that we must not disregard.

In order to make some of these concepts more concrete, imagine a human who is in love with ants. Such a person condescends, reveals, and covenants with an ant farm. The human physically lowers himself to speak to ants, reveals information about himself, makes promises of how he will provide for them, and has expectations for how they should live. In this silly example, we might think that this is an exaggeration of the CREATOR-creature Distinction, but in a way, it is too mild! For ants and humans are under the same category of fellow creatures. The independent CREATOR, however, is categorically different than his creation.[8] An important motif is that God wants his people to reciprocate his gracious acts of condescension, revelation, and covenant by trusting in him. It is from this genuine trust that obedience and adoration generate so that we can, like David, confess, "What is man that you are mindful of him, and the son of man that you care for him?" (Ps 8:4; see also Ps 144:3).[9]

---

7. For a fuller treatment on this rich concept, see Block, *Covenant*.

8. Like any illustration, this one breaks down because humanity is created in the image of God. But being created in the image of God is something that God graciously bestows upon humanity, so it should not be used to downplay the unexpected love of God condescending, revealing, and covenanting with humanity.

9. Throughout this book, I use the word "trust" rather than "believe" or "faith" to emphasize the relational and submissive qualities that are often minimized—trust is highlighted in Scripture because it points outside of ourselves (the creature domain) and to God's character and promises and ultimately Christ (the CREATOR domain). The original Greek and Latin words (*pistis* and *fides*)—from which we get words like "believe," "trust," and "faith"—have a very pervasive role in the ancient Mediterranean context of the New Testament. These words express something relational more than a set of beliefs or a matter within the heart/mind. They serve as the underpinnings of all relationships, but the New Testament uses these ideas in fascinating ways, primarily in one's relationship with God. For a detailed study on this, see Morgan, *Roman Faith*. This understanding of "faith," "believe," and "trust" is similar to how John Murray explains how the nature

As our awareness of God's majesty and the immense blessings he lavishes upon us increases, we gain a more accurate comprehension of the folly and wickedness of sin. The story of Scripture, therefore, now progresses to the next biblical principle: the Problem of Sin.

THE PROBLEM OF SIN

Implications: The Template for All Temptations

Instead of trusting, obeying, and adoring their CREATOR, we earlier saw in Gen 3:1–6 that the serpent tempts Adam and Eve to distort, suppress, and reject God's character and promises. God's laws are for their benefit and are reminders of his generosity; yet instead they twist these laws. On the left column is the reality of the laws and how humanity should have responded to God's gracious revelation; on the right is how they regrettably distorted, suppressed, and ultimately rejected God:

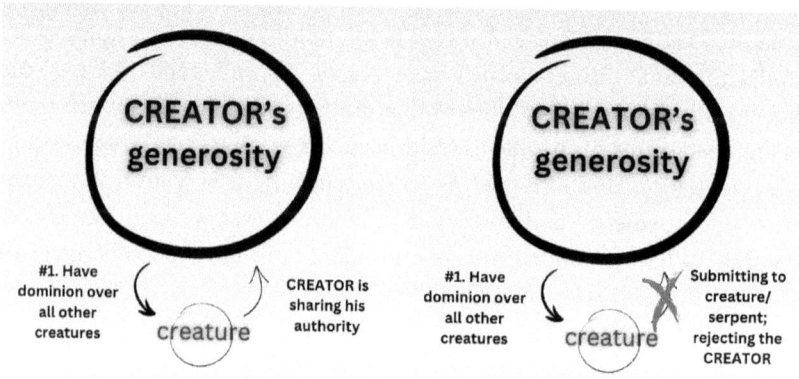

---

of faith must include knowledge, conviction, and trust (*Redemption Accomplished and Applied*, 115–18). As noted in chapter 1, it is from this trust that obedience flows.

Defining the Approach

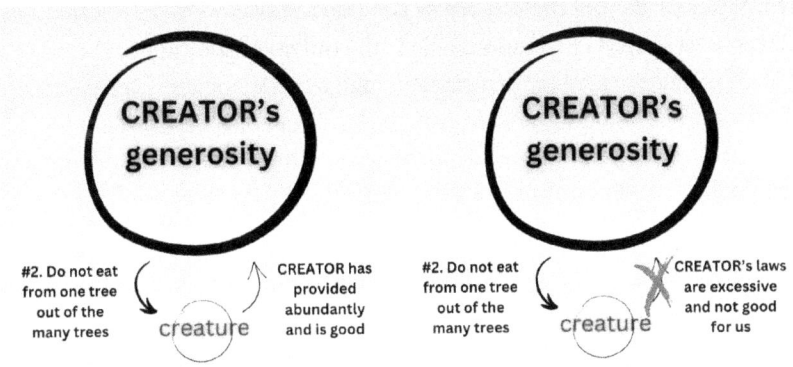

This temptation, however, is not an isolated example. In fact, this is the very template for all temptations because sin at its core is a distrust of God's character or promises. While Gen 3:1–6 explains this in the form of a suspenseful narrative, Paul later explains it in the form of a logical argument (Rom 1:18–32).

This template is most clearly seen in well-known accounts like the golden calf debacle (Exod 32), as well as the temptation of Jesus (Luke 4:1–13)—both we later explore in greater detail. However, this template should be seen in every other temptation recorded in Scripture. As a result, we see more clearly what the root of the problem is in each passage. This chapter ends with concrete steps so that we can apply them ourselves.

As the subtitle of this book suggests, when we begin to diagnose the root of the problem of each passage, we are then able to do the same in our own lives. Understanding His word as intended means we will less likely be preoccupied with external symptoms of sin and instead be more cognizant of the essence of sin. At its essence, sin is relational, specifically against God—because the relationship with God is broken, the symptoms of sin that destroy the self and other relationships follow.[10] If we are unable to see this distinction, the essence of sin is erroneously reduced to its symptoms, such as sexual immorality, addictions, or whatever is trending in society. Consequently, we settle for a "gospel" that is nothing more than self-help or behavior modification.[11] If we are able to see this distinction between the

---

10. To be more accurate, it is "anti-relational." Gaffin, *By Faith*, 30–33.

11. Thus, Murray writes, "In the last analysis sin is always against *God*, and the essence of sin is to be *against* God." *Redemption Accomplished and Applied*, 123; italics original. For a similar idea expounded further, see Herman Ridderbos (*Paul*, 100–107) who describes sins as enmity against God (so, primarily "theological") that produces many consequences (so as a result, "anthropological").

symptoms of sin and the essence of sin, then a meaningful dependence on Christ arises in every situation, who is the only true solution to sin.

It is therefore fitting that immediately after Adam and Eve's fall to sin, the promises of redemption are given by God—all of which develop organically in Scripture and ultimately foreshadow Christ. In the face of guilt and shame, Scripture points us to Christ.

THE ORGANISM OF SCRIPTURE

The previous chapter mentioned the devastating consequences of sin. Because of Adam's unique role as the federal head, every aspect of creation that has been entrusted to Adam has been corrupted. Humans are now spiritually dead and born with a sinful nature. Although these are the consequences of sin, God unexpectedly extends promises of redemption in the face of this rebellion. All these promises are developed throughout the rest of Scripture, which culminate in Christ. Hence, Scripture is not a compilation of random stories, arbitrary rules, and miscellaneous prayers. Instead, there is an organic connection between all the parts, all of which lead to Christ.

To make the Organism of Scripture more understandable and applicable, the following subsections explain three important concepts: the *literary flow* of Scripture, the *covenantal/iterative flow* of Scripture, and the *death and resurrection of Christ*. As a result, we will see the connection to the death and resurrection of Christ more meaningfully and organically.

Literary Flow

Scripture consists of the Old and New Testaments. Foundational to the Old Testament are the first five books of the Bible: Genesis, Exodus, Leviticus, Numbers, and Deuteronomy. These books are often referred to as the Pentateuch, the Law of Moses, or the Torah. The reason why these books are foundational is that they outline God's character and promises. All the other Old Testament books are asking the questions: Will the people of God live according to his character and promises? Will they trust him or continually distort, suppress, or reject him?[12]

---

12. As we saw in the previous chapter and will see in the next, these questions are relevant in the Pentateuch as well.

Defining the Approach

1. The thirteen historical books (Joshua to 2 Chronicles) make it painfully clear that God's people do not live according to his character and promises, and continually reject him from the perspective of the history of Israel.

2. The five books of the wisdom literature or the Writings (Job, Psalms, Proverbs, Ecclesiastes, and Song of Solomon) communicate an unsettling ambivalence to the Torah in the form of poetry and biblical principles. The ambivalence is not because there is anything wrong with God's word—these books recognize both the wisdom to live according to the CREATOR-creature Distinction and their inability to do so because of the Problem of Sin.

3. The seventeen prophetic books (Isaiah to Malachi) answer these questions quite emphatically through prophetic proclamation: the people of God relentlessly fail to trust God.

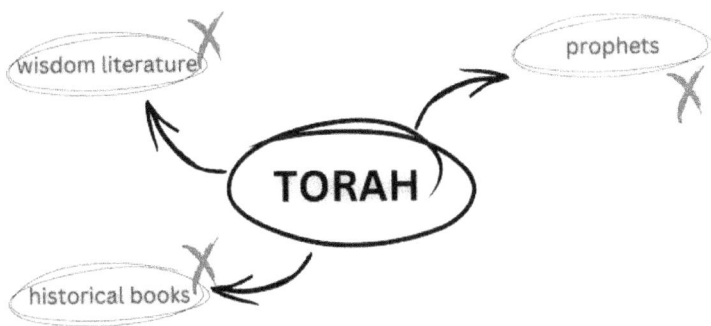

Thus, the diagram depicts the heliocentric role that the Torah has on the rest of the Old Testament.[13] Over again, no matter how faithful God is, his people blatantly spurn his love and faithfulness. The tension is quite tedious, repetitive, and frustrating. But, as Paul writes later, Israel is a spiritual mirror to us, so all these examples reinforce that God is the faithful main character of *our* lives despite *our* perpetual failure to trust him (1 Cor 10:1–6; see also Heb 3:7—4:13). We are able to exhale a sigh of relief when we get to the New Testament.

The New Testament begins with the four Gospels. These Gospels introduce an individual who is both unlike and similar to all the side characters of the Old Testament: Jesus Christ. While the Gospel writers portray

---

13. This point is even clearer in the Hebrew Bible, which divides the books differently (i.e., Torah, Prophets or *Nevi'im*, and Writings or *Ketuvim*).

Jesus to evoke memories of Adam, Abraham, Moses, Israel, and others, he is also strikingly unique. Jesus answers the questions of living according to God's character and promises with a resounding yes. Jesus trusts the Father perfectly. He is the exact embodiment of the righteousness and glory of God, fulfilling all of Torah as intended.

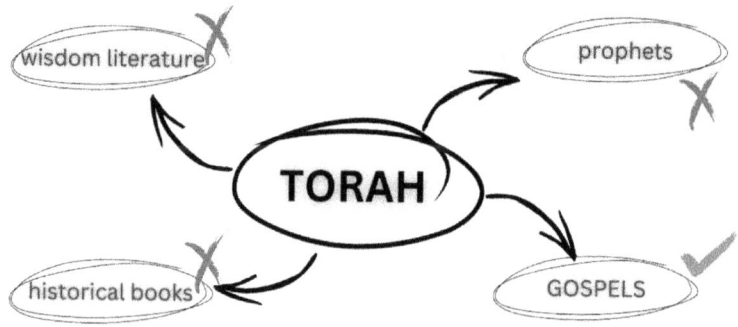

However, there is a paradigm shift. Rather than all of Scripture revolving around the Torah, we learn that all of Scripture actually revolves around Jesus himself!

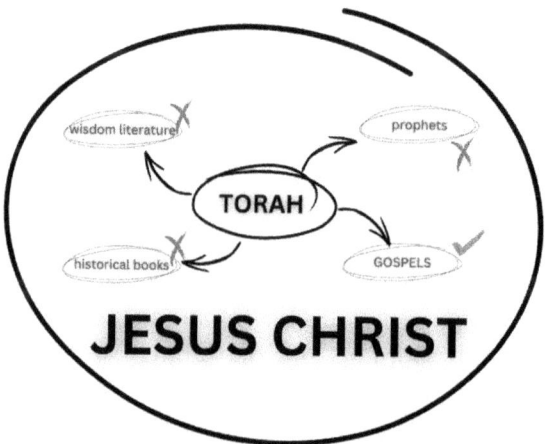

Thus the rest of the New Testament raises the same questions but answers them differently:

1. The Acts of the Apostles is a historical account of how the *first church* trusted in God's character and promises despite constant persecution.

Defining the Approach

2. The twenty-one Epistles (Romans to Jude) explain that the *everyday church* can live according to his character and promises in the form of biblical principles.[14]

3. Revelation expresses the same assurance that the *last church* will remain faithful in the form of a prophetic or apocalyptic vision.[15]

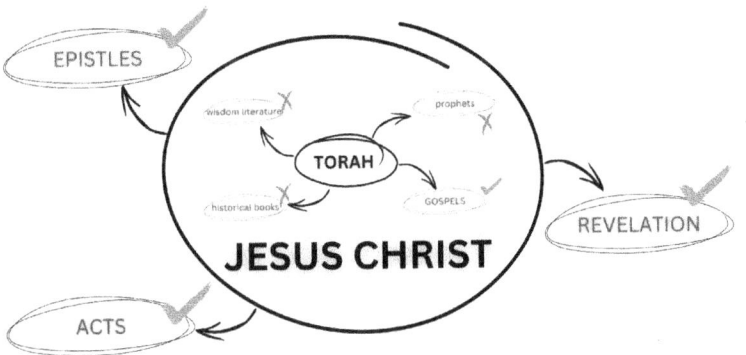

What, then, is the difference between the people of God of the Old and New Testaments? Ultimately, it is the death and resurrection of Christ. We will unpack some of the implications of the death and resurrection below, but what is central is his people are now united with Christ. Since Christ never failed and his Spirit is in his people forever, his people will not fail. Hence, the difference has less to do with the people (i.e., the side characters) and

---

14. Vos's explanation on the relation between the Epistles and the Gospels is applied throughout this book:

> As a matter of fact, He does not represent Himself anywhere as being by his human earthly activity the exhaustive expounder of truth. Much rather He is the great fact to be expounded. . . . For this reason the teaching of Jesus, so far from rendering the teaching of the Apostles negligible, absolutely postulates it. As the latter would have been empty, lacking the fact, so the former would have been blind, at least in part, because of lacking the light. The relation between Jesus and the Apostolate is in general that between the fact to be interpreted and the subsequent interpretation of this fact. This is none other than the principle under which all revelation proceeds. (*Biblical Theology*, 324–25)

Thus, there is no contradiction between what some people refer to as the gospel or Christianity of Jesus and the gospel or Christianity of Paul. My students have appreciated the metaphor that I use: the Gospels are the meme while the Epistles are the caption for that meme.

15. Much more nuance can be provided. As a helpful starting point, see Kruger, *Biblical-Theological Introduction*. Relatedly, a common question is how to interpret the problems in the church. The distinction between the invisible and visible church is a helpful starting point. But the emphasis is not to place our confidence in the church or the people of God, but in the person and work of Christ.

everything to do with Jesus (i.e., the main character). The literary flow reminds us that every road of Scripture—whether a census from Numbers or an obscure saying from Ecclesiastes—leads to Christ.[16]

Covenantal/Iterative Flow

Another important concept related to the Organism of Scripture is covenant. All of Scripture is full of a consistent pattern: *indicatives, imperatives,* and *fulfillment*. Seeing this pattern throughout Scripture shows why sin and temptation are so effective. Moreover, it helps us see Christ more consistently.[17]

According to the *Britannica*, an "indicative" as a noun is "the form that a verb or sentence has when it is stating a fact that can be known or proved."[18] I use indicatives to convey completed actions or facts, most of which pertain to God's character or promises. Scripture therefore overflows with indicatives. For instance, most of the passages we explored in the previous chapter (Gen 1–3) are indicatives: who God is, what he has done, what he promised will happen, etc. Every covenant begins with indicatives.[19] In fact, the CREATOR-creature Distinction is the primordial indicative. In order for us to enjoy these indicatives, we need imperatives.

Imperatives are commands, but in Scripture, they are more invitations or privileges, as we saw in the previous chapter. God commands or invites his people to live according to the indicatives. It is crucial to recognize that imperatives flow out of the indicatives. Genesis 1–3 are written in a way to display a pattern: it is because God created humanity in his image and gave them authority (indicative) that they are to have dominion over his

---

16. The purpose of this book is to provide examples and an approach to see this reality throughout the Old Testament. See also Van Pelt, *Gospel Promised*.

17. Although "indicatives" and "imperatives" are concepts introduced by others in the past (e.g., Ridderbos, *Paul*, 253–58), there are differences and similarities in how I am using them. The similarities are that imperatives must flow from the indicatives and that both indicatives and imperatives are grounded in a trust/faith in God. The differences are that I am using these terms not only in the New Testament Epistles but all of Scripture, and that I am adding another concept, "fulfillment," to show how Scripture emphasizes the failures of God's people, which sets up the perfect fulfillment that Christ accomplishes and shares with his people through his death and resurrection.

18. *Britannica*, s.v. "indicative," accessed June 19, 2025, https://www.britannica.com/dictionary/indicative.

19. In ancient Near Eastern covenants, these would be the preamble and prologue.

Defining the Approach

beautiful creation (imperative); and it is because God abundantly provided humanity attractive and good food (indicative) that they are not to eat from a specified tree (imperative). Once we focus on the imperative at the expense of the indicative, distrusting God is crouching at the door.

Fulfillment asks and answers the question, did the people of God respond to his indicatives as intended? Were they faithful to the imperative? If yes, then they are blessed because they are enjoying and living according to the glorious indicatives. If no, then they should expect the consequences of failed imperatives. The story of Scripture shows that the people of God are persistently ignoring the indicatives, spurning the imperatives, and therefore failing the fulfillment.

If an imperative is rejected, then there is a need to address not only the consequence of that rejection but the original requirement of that imperative. For instance, if an employee misses the deadline of an important task, the employee needs to address the consequence of the missed deadline *and* complete the original task. Thus, there are two needs associated with these failures: the *consequences* of sin and the *requirements* of God.[20] We will see momentarily that these concepts help us to understand and appreciate why Scripture stresses both the death and resurrection of Christ (e.g., Luke 24:46; Rom 4:25; 1 Cor 2:2, 15:3–4; etc.).

Despite the countless failures recorded in Scripture, God graciously responds to each of them with more indicatives! Rather than meting out the full weight of his righteous judgment, he withholds it and offers more mercy. If the first indicative-imperative-fulfillment triad is broken in Gen 3:1–6, then God wraps it around another set of indicatives, offering another set of imperatives, but only to see this fulfillment failed yet again. This is precisely what happens in Gen 3:7–24 and becomes an iterative pattern throughout the rest of Scripture. He continually wraps the failures of his people around another indicative-imperative-fulfillment triad. In this way, all of the Old Testament is like a growing Russian doll set.

The following two diagrams illustrate this point. The first is more explicit while the second is more visual. In each, the broken triad is wrapped by another triad iteratively. This is why they are numbered 1, 2, and eventually "n"—God wraps around the first broken triad ("1") with a second ("2"), which is broken only to be wrapped around countless more ("n")

---

20. For a fuller treatment on this—including how this intersects with the active and passive obedience of Christ, the two benefits of justification (i.e., the forgiveness of sins and the right to eternal life), and the sins of omission and commission—see Crowe, *Perfect Life*, 15–57.

until Christ finally fulfills everything—both the *consequences* of sin and the *requirements* of God. In the second diagram, we see that this iteration is not merely neutral, as if the repeated defiance against God hovers on a straight line. Instead, there is a downward descent.

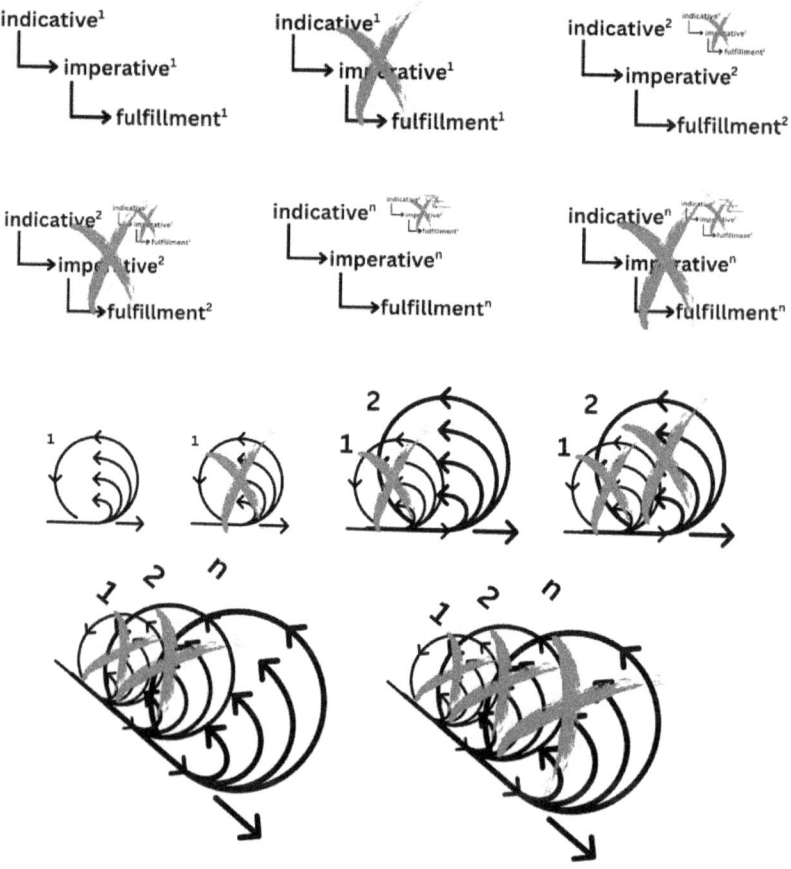

The Death and Resurrection of Christ

Although the covenantal/iterative flow might seem unnecessary or abstract, it highlights important details of Scripture that we otherwise overlook and—most importantly—the relevance of the death and resurrection of Christ. Scripture reveals countless broken indicative-imperative-fulfillment triads in order to alert our attention to the growing need to address both the consequences of sin and the requirements of God, which can only be satisfied by the death and resurrection of Christ. Reading the Old Testament raises at least a couple of questions. On the one hand, if God is perfectly righteous, then what happens to all the failed fulfillments of his people? On the other hand, there are instances where God's people do fulfill his imperatives through trust and obedience—how are we to interpret these?

An important verse that we see later from the New Testament by Paul is a great starting point: Jesus "was *delivered up for our trespasses* and **raised for our justification**" (Rom 4:25). Let's unpack this verse in light of these questions. Although the death and resurrection of Christ cannot be separated, it is helpful to punctuate each aspect so that we can more fully appreciate the work of Christ.[21]

The Death of Christ

The italicized text (*"delivered up for our trespasses"*) accents the death of Christ, which addresses the consequences of sin accumulated by the failed imperatives.

Every failure must be accounted. Although Moses is prohibited from reaching the promised land (Num 20:12), Gideon falls into arrogance and pride (Judg 8), and David commits adultery and murder (2 Sam 11), none of these individuals receive the full consequences of their sins. The people of God have therefore incurred an incalculable invoice containing countless line items. Part of understanding Scripture as intended is developing a growing frustration and an increasing anticipation for some kind of resolution.

All these failures mount iteratively like a Russian doll set until they are shockingly and satisfactorily paid in full by the death of Christ. Christ trusts, submits to, and obeys the Father even to the point of dying on a cross—the most humiliating form of execution in the Greco-Roman world. Thus, Christ takes the full consequences of the sins of his people. Scripture regards the period before the death of Christ as one of forbearance: God is "overlooking" the sins of his people not because he ignores them, for he

---

21. As Calvin instructs, "So then, let us remember that whenever mention is made of his death alone, we are to understand at the same time what belongs to his resurrection. Also, the same synecdoche applies to the word 'resurrection': whenever it is mentioned separately from death, we are to understand it as including what has to do especially with his death." *Institutes*, 2.16.13.

is perfectly righteous and just, but because they are to be addressed by the death of Christ (Acts 17:30, Rom 3:25).[22]

The Resurrection of Christ

The emboldened text ("**raised for our justification**") accents the resurrection of Christ. His resurrection is linked to our justification, which is roughly synonymous with righteousness. If the death addresses the consequences of sin, then his resurrection addresses the requirements of God that his people failed to meet.

This, along with many other verses in Scripture, imply that all the instances where God's people do fulfill one or some of his imperatives are never sufficient to satisfy God's ultimate requirements.[23] Some of these instances are quite inspirational. In the ancient Near East, Abram's willingness to leave the distant land of Ur to an unknown land is an extraordinary expression of trust in God (Gen 11:27—12:4). Joseph forgiving his brothers for attempting to murder him and eventually selling him into slavery is commendatory (e.g., Gen 50:15–21).

However, even the most heroic acts of obedience cannot satisfy the requirements of God. Christ, on the other hand, does satisfy these requirements perfectly. Every nanosecond of his life, Christ obeyed the will of the Father—and this not merely for his own sake but for his enemies (e.g., Rom 5:10). Thus, Christ did not merely obey the Father and fulfill all righteousness with his death, but with the entirety of his life.[24] This is one of the reasons why the Gospels include details of his baptism; the way he loved, taught, and healed others; and—most fundamentally—how he always trusted and submitted to the Father while relying on the Spirit. Part of the reason why the blood of Jesus is so effective is that he lived in perfect righteousness, rendering his role as the sacrificial lamb blameless (Heb 9:14;

---

22. On the significance of the death of Christ, see Murray, *Redemption Accomplished and Applied*, 14–48.

23. A counterpoint might be Gen 15:6. While a full treatment cannot be provided here, the reason why Abram's trust is highlighted is that trust is relational and submissive. Therefore, trust points outside of ourselves to God's character and promises, and ultimately Christ. Abram's instance of trust also generates obedience (see n. 9 above). So Paul and James later explain this dynamic from different vantage points (e.g., Rom 4:1–12, Jas 2:18–26).

24. For an extensive treatment on this, see Crowe, *Perfect Life*.

Defining the Approach

1 Pet 1:19; see also Exod 12:5). Hence, Jesus does what no other human can do: he perfectly fulfills the requirements of God.

One of the purposes of these positive instances in the Old Testament is that they foreshadow the perfect righteousness of Christ. If the sins accumulated in the Old Testament provide a deeper context, background, and meaning for the death of Christ, then the positive instances of trust provide the same for his righteousness. A greater understanding of the side characters is designed to cultivate a deeper appreciation for the main character.[25] So if Abram leaving his familiar home of Ur to an unspecified territory was a tall task, how much more Christ, who selflessly incarnated as his own creation, being born in the form of a servant (Phil 2:6–8)? If Joseph forgiving his brothers for their treacherous plot is admirable, how much more glorious is it that Christ forgives his own creation who repeatedly hate and reject him (e.g., John 1:10–11)?

But what does the righteousness of Christ have to do with his resurrection? It is in his resurrection that Christ is officially declared righteous (e.g., Rom 1:4, 1 Tim 3:16).[26] His resurrection, among other things, proves that the entirety of his life perfectly addresses God's requirements and that he did not deserve death. All this he does for *our* salvation—"*our trespasses*" and "**our justification**" (Rom 4:25). So returning to the verse that we are currently unpacking (Rom 4:25), his resurrection is not only the official declaration of his righteousness and justification but the official declaration of ours ("**raised for our justification**"). As all the failures of God's people find their endpoint in the death of Christ, all the acts of obedience find their endpoint in his resurrection.

Jesus, the True Adam

This is one of many reasons why the death and resurrection of Christ are not only central in Scripture but in the life of a Christian.[27] They not only reverse the catastrophic consequences of Adam's sin, but they afford

---

25. Thus, the approach in this book shares the underlying principles of the redemptive-historical approach that takes covenant seriously. In the context of preaching, see Clowney, *Preaching Christ*, 11–44; Johnson, *Him We Proclaim*, 230–38.

26. On the resurrection being the justification of Christ, see Gaffin, *Resurrection and Redemption*, 119–24.

27. "The Christian life in its entirety is to be subsumed under the category of resurrection. Pointedly, the Christian life is the resurrection-life." Gaffin, *By Faith*, 68.

blessings that Adam never obtained. While the sin of one federal head produces death for many, the death and resurrection of the other federal head produces life for many (Rom 5:12–21). While Adam's sin has a cascading impact on all of humanity, the death and resurrection have a cascading impact for those in Christ. The impact that the death and resurrection of Christ has on us is at least threefold:[28]

1. Because of his death, his people have the forgiveness of all their sins—past, present, and future. This satisfies the *consequences* of sin that his people accumulated.

2. Because of his resurrection, the righteousness of Christ is shared with his people in two ways:

   a. The Father declares his people to be righteous. Thus, the righteousness of Christ is imputed to his people, satisfying the *requirements* of God that they never met on their own.[29]

   b. The Spirit conforms his people to the righteousness of Christ. Thus, they are gradually being transformed to embody the righteousness of Christ.

So when God views us who are in Christ, he sees *both* the blood of Christ that washes all our sin (death) *and* the righteousness of Christ that clothes us (resurrection)—satisfying *both* the consequences of sin *and* the requirements of God. Some of us might wish that we could have the righteousness of the side characters of Scripture—for instance, Moses, who is Israel's greatest leader, or Job, who is blameless before God. Instead, God *both* imputes to us *and* conforms us to the righteousness of *Christ* (Phil 3:9)!

---

28. The most central implication is our union with Christ and the permanent dwelling of the Spirit, which I plan to be my next project.

29. The verb "impute" generally comes from the Greek *logizomai* (e.g., Rom 4:3). The primary glosses from the LSJ (the Liddell, Scott, and Jones *Greek-English Lexicon*) are "count, reckon," which imply a definitive, objective, or mathematical decision (LSJ, s.v. "λογίζομα," 1055). In the New Testament context, it is used to convey something declarative, legal, or forensic. One of the reasons that the LSJ is a valuable lexicon for New Testament studies is that it draws upon *all* Greek texts from antiquity so that we can understand how these words were perceived and used by Greek speaker/hearers. For more details, especially how "impute" differs significantly from "infuse," see Crowe, *Perfect Life*, 27–31.

Since the relationship between the resurrection of Christ and our righteousness can be difficult to remember, the table and diagram summarize these points within the indicative-imperative-fulfillment triad:[30]

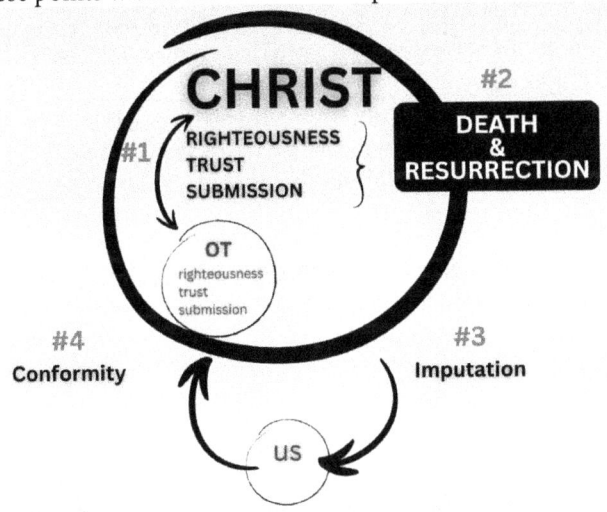

#1	**Old Testament ⇔ Christ:**	
	All the instances of trust, submission, and righteousness in the Old Testament foreshadow the perfect righteousness of Christ; Christ is the fulfillment of the Old Testament. This deepens our appreciation for the righteousness of Christ that he shares with his people.	Indicative
#2a	**Death of Christ:**	
	The perfect obedience of Christ is necessary for the efficacy of his death to pay the consequences of the sins of all his people.	Indicative
#2b	**Resurrection of Christ:**	
	The resurrection of Christ is the official declaration of his perfect obedience and the injustice of his death.	Indicative
#3	**Imputation:**	
	Because his people are united to Christ, his righteousness is imputed to them. His people are officially and legally declared righteous by the Father, satisfying the requirements of God.	Indicative

---

30. This is merely a slice of what Christ has done and how it relates with us. This is what theologians call the *ordo salutis* and the *historia salutis*. For a fuller treatment, see Murray, *Redemption Accomplished and Applied*.

#4	**Conformity:** His people are being transformed progressively and gradually to the righteousness of Christ by the Spirit. The righteousness of Christ is most clearly revealed in both the Old and New Testaments. These are the scripts to which his people are being conformed.	**Imperative**
	Part of the promise that Christ has secured for his people is that he will complete the good work that he has begun in us through the permanent dwelling of his Spirit.	**Fulfillment**

THE ORGANIC AND MEANINGFUL CONNECTION TO CHRIST

Summary

The three biblical principles of this approach provide the essential context to understand every passage of Scripture. The CREATOR-creature Distinction reminds us that God's word is primarily about God—specifically his character and promises. Accordingly, God—not Abraham, Moses, David, Peter, Paul, or even the church—is the main character of every passage. Moreover, the aspects of God's character and promises revealed in Scripture are overwhelming. He is full of love, righteousness, benevolence, generosity, faithfulness, patience, and every other virtue. His promises are surprising, undeserving, extravagant, comprehensive, and certain. His laws are less demands and more invitations to relish in his good character and promises.

Yet, we might struggle to see the prominence and beauty of God in both the passages that we read and the scenarios of our everyday life. If we read Scripture as if the side characters are the main characters, then we will live our own life as if we are the main character. Furthermore, when we do reflect upon who God is, rather than being arrested by his majesty and love, we sometimes feel an excessive, unhealthy, or unreasonable burden. The way that Adam and Eve mistake God's provisions and commands is how we misconstrue God's character and promises. The Problem of Sin, therefore, brings our attention to a baffling dynamic that is entwined in the fabric of Scripture: as much as the Bible is replete with the goodness of God, it also amply attests humanity's irrational, egregious, wanton, and incessant rejection of God's character and promises. Scripture therefore enraptures us by pointing us to who God is while simultaneously exposing our obstinate refusal to acknowledge and live according to who God is.

What hope, then, is there for Abraham, Moses, David, Peter, Paul, the church, or us? Although this is the crucial question, it is seldomly reflected upon in a way that organically and meaningfully displays Christ. Rather, we often settle for solutions that are secondary. For instance, we need more effective accountability in our relationships with others, we need to be more disciplined with our devotionals, we need to be more active in our evangelism, we need to be more involved in the church, we need to be more understanding and loving, and so on.

While there is much wisdom in these examples, the Creator-creature Distinction and the Problem of Sin help us to see that these solutions cannot be primary or fundamental. Most of these examples, in fact, are human- or self-generated—that is, their motivation and source are not grounded in Christ. The Organism of Scripture, however, disciplines us to see every passage—and eventually every moment of our lives—in the light of Christ. The literary flow of Scripture reminds us that every part of the Bible finds its hope in Christ; the covenantal/iterative flow of Scripture shows that every part of the Bible consists of the indicative-imperative-fulfillment triad, which is only fulfilled in Christ; and the death and resurrection of Christ offer true hope because they alone address both the consequences of our sin and the requirements of God that we cannot meet.[31] Christ alone is the one who lived in worshipful trust and submission to the Father. And his Spirit alone is the one who enables us to live life as intended. This fundamental solution is the motivation and source to be able to grow in accountability, discipline, evangelism, church, love, and so on. Failure to recognize this is to misdiagnose the root problem, leading to spiritual malpractice.

Diagram and Table for Application

Thus, these three principles are vital in being able to read Scripture and live life as intended—so that in every passage and in all things, our hope is in Christ alone.[32] By understanding and applying the concepts of this book,

---

31. Goldsworthy succinctly writes, "If Christ truly is our Lord and Saviour, then he is the Lord and Saviour of our hermeneutics." *Gospel-Centered Hermeneutics*, 19.

32. In addition to chapter 1's treatment on Gen 1–3, this book contains many other examples of how these three principles not only repeat throughout Scripture, but help us understand Scripture as written and intended. In addition to those examples, here are

a simple point emerges: we are sinning more than we realize because we are not always recognizing the reality that God is always revealing himself to us, so therefore we are always at the mercy of God, which is most fully expressed in the death and resurrection of Christ. Below is a diagram that is a helpful starting point for how to apply these concepts to narratives:

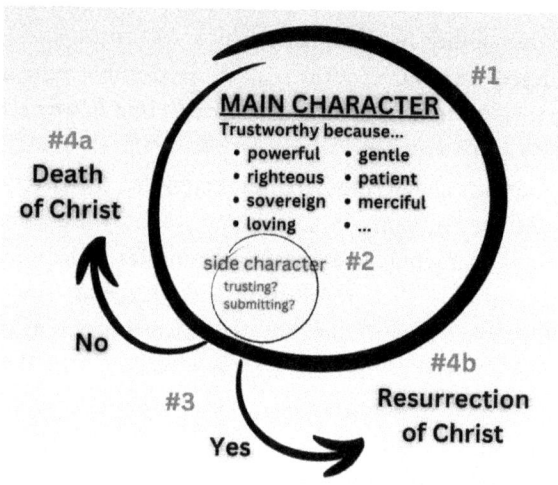

two glaring ones at key junctures of Scripture: Psalm 1 and the prologue to the Gospel of John. For Ps 1: (a) Ps 1:1–3—the CREATOR-creature Distinction: the blessed live according to the CREATOR-creature Distinction and therefore flourish, unlike what we saw in Adam and what we will see in Israel; (b) Ps 1:4–5—the Problem of Sin: the wicked resist the CREATOR-creature Distinction by distorting, suppressing, and rejecting the character and promises of God; and (c) Ps 1:5–6—the Organism of Scripture: the final judgment is executed by Christ, wherein the decisive factor is whether people trusted or rejected the testimony of Scripture. Those who trusted in Christ's death and resurrection will be vindicated by his blood and righteousness, while those who have not will perish. For John: (a) John 1:1–4, 9—the CREATOR-creature Distinction: this is an allusion to the creation account of Gen 1–2 where all good things find their existence in the independent CREATOR; (b) John 1:5, 10–11—the Problem of Sin: despite God being the source of all good things and reaching out to his creation, his creation nonetheless distorts, suppresses, and ultimately rejects him; and (c) John 1:6–8, 12–18—the Organism of Scripture: the witness of Scripture, including the roles of John the Baptist, the law, and Moses, are essentially about Christ, especially his death and resurrection. Note that the phrase "dwelt among us" (1:14) is literally "tabernacled in us" (from the uncommon verb *skēnoō*), which brings to view both the tabernacle and union with Christ (a topic that I hope to explain further in a separate project).

Defining the Approach

#1	**Main Character's Trustworthiness:** In this narrative passage, what reasons are given to trust God? What aspects of God's character and promises are relevant? The passage or the context of the passage will provide specific reasons why God is trustworthy. *In Gen 1–2, some of these reasons included the way God creates, provides for, and loves humanity.*	Indicative
#2	**Main Character's Invitation:** How is God inviting the side characters to trust him? What are the specific imperatives, and what is God's tone in the invitation? In the light of the ample reasons to trust God (#1), God is inviting the side characters to trust in him—his character and promises. Remember, as the independent CREATOR, he has no need for side characters. The invitation or imperative is a gracious example of him condescending, revealing, and covenanting with his people. *In Gen 1–3, God gives Adam and Eve gracious imperatives that are invitations to live according to God's abundant generosity.*	Imperative
#3	**Side Character's Response:** How do the side characters respond? Do they recognize the indicatives? Do they ignore the character and promises of God that are revealed? The narrative shows if the side characters respond in trust/submission or distrust/rejection. *In Gen 3:1–6, Adam and Eve distort, suppress, and reject God's character and promises; instead they place their trust in the serpent.*	Fulfillment
#4	**Christ's Fulfillment:** How does this passage enrich our appreciation for the death and resurrection of Christ? In what ways does this passage provide more context to the death and resurrection of Christ? Christ fulfills the imperative in two ways: a. Christ fulfills the *consequences* of failing the imperative on behalf of his people through his death. Thus, the failure of his people is tolerated by God.[33] b. Christ fulfills the *requirements* of following the imperative by perfectly trusting and obeying God. The trust from his people foreshadows the perfect righteousness of Christ. This righteousness is shared with his people through his resurrection: the Father declares his people to be righteous in Christ, and the Spirit conforms his people to embody the righteousness of Christ (see the diagram on the resurrection and righteousness of Christ on pp. 45–46). *In Gen 3:7–24, Adam's failure points to #4a, and the four promises that God makes point to #4b.*	Fulfillment

---

33. As we see in chapter 5 (Rev 19–22), all other sins will be addressed at the return of Jesus.

NEXT STEPS

At this point in Scripture, there are two issues that consistently derail us from understanding it as intended. The first is the failure to see the coherence of all the narratives. Between Gen 3 and Exod 19, there are many different personalities, stories, and developments. Some of them are quite fascinating, others seem arbitrary. However, this is only because we erroneously make the side characters into the main character. So the approach outlined in this chapter (as well as the example from chapter 1) are intended for readers to apply this approach to the passages between Gen 3 and Exod 19 (most of these passages are in narrative). As a result, the seemingly random stories between Gen 3 and Exod 19 converge to exhibit *the* story and *the* main character.

The second issue is misunderstanding the deliverance of Israel's slavery from Egypt (Exod 1–18). The purpose of the deliverance is explained explicitly by God through the Mosaic covenant, law, and tabernacle (Exod 19–40)—all of which we either misconstrue or overlook. Applying this approach enables us to see the richness of these concepts and how each of them points to Christ. All of this is the focus of the next chapter.

Lastly if the Problem of Sin means that we are hopelessly distorting, suppressing, and rejecting God's character or promises, then no book, diagram, or instructions can address the problem. The fundamental problem is sin, so the fundamental solution is the gospel of Christ. Therefore, being able to understand Scripture as intended, let alone having the desire to do so and the power to live according to it, is only possible through Christ. Thankfully, Christ has given us his Spirit so that we can have the desire to read his word, understand it as intended, and live according to it (e.g., John 14:26; 1 Cor 2:10–16; Eph 1:15–19, 3:14–19). Therefore, praying before, during, and after every engagement with Scripture is a vital expression of our need and desire for the Spirit.[34]

QUESTIONS FOR REFLECTION AND PRAYER

a. The chapter begins by stressing the importance of not only the three biblical principles (the CREATOR-creature Distinction, the Problem of

---

34. For more details on this as it pertains to hermeneutics, see Goldsworthy, *Gospel-Centered Hermeneutics*, 39–85; G. K. Beale, "New Testament Hermeneutics," in Lillback, *Seeing Christ*, 32–34; Poythress, *Reading the Word*, 403–16.

Sin, and the Organism of Scripture) but the specific sequence. In your own words, explain why these principles are important, especially in this sequence.

b. Reflect upon the CREATOR-creature Distinction, especially how the independent CREATOR graciously condescends, reveals, and covenants with us. What do they mean for you personally? Pray that the Spirit will make your engagement with Scripture help you to be more aware of these blessings.

c. How does the covenantal/iterative flow (indicative-imperative-fulfillment triad) make sense of some of the tension building in the Old Testament? More importantly, how does the covenantal/iterative flow deepen your appreciation for what Christ has done for you?

d. Why are all three of the implications of the death and resurrection of Christ covered in this chapter necessary? Which implication(s) do you often underappreciate?

   1. The Son's blood cleanses us of all sins—past, present, and future (the consequences of sin).

   2. The Father declares us to be righteous because we are in Christ (the requirements of God).

   3. The Spirit conforms us to the righteousness of Christ.

e. Try applying the narrative diagram on one or all the following passages: Gen 11:27—12:8, 12:10-20, 3:1—4:17; Exod 14:1-31, 16:1-36.

3

Christ as the True Israel (Exod 19–20, 24)

STAYING AT DIFFERENT AIRBNBS makes a biblical principle even more concrete. The rules and décor of the house can reveal something about the landlord. In some, the housekeeping rules are relational. They include jokes, emojis, or even a picture of the landlord and the family. The furniture, decoration, and even the board games provided all convey the relationality of the landlord. In others, the rules are terse, and the only details provided are the consequences of broken rules. Only the most necessary items are furnished without any effort toward aesthetics or recreation.

In this pivotal portion of Scripture, God reveals his rules (known as the Torah or the Law of Moses) and the décor of his abode (known as the tabernacle), all of which is in the context of a covenant (known as the Mosaic covenant). Just like how we hijack narratives, we often get fixated on the details of the laws without recognizing what they say about their landlord. If anything, we typically misconstrue these laws as burdensome or irrelevant, often assuming that God is unfair. As we saw in chapter 1, this is exactly what happened in Gen 3:1–6 with Adam and Eve; as we saw in chapter 2, this is the template to sin and temptation.

The CREATOR-creature Distinction, however, reminds us that all of reality, including laws, is an expression of God's gracious condescension, revelation, and covenant with us. The independent God has no need for these laws or even for us to obey them; they are given for our benefit.

Christ as the True Israel (Exod 19–20, 24)

Although all of reality, including laws, reveals God's character and promises, the Problem of Sin means that we make his revelation about something else by distorting, suppressing, and rejecting him. Thus, we are at the utter mercies of God not only to give us the motivation to read his word but the ability to understand it as intended and to live according to it—all of which is possible only by the Holy Spirit, who has been given to us through the death and resurrection of Christ.

As the Spirit helps us, we see that there is an Organism of Scripture. Laws or details about the tabernacle are not random, but they are pieces to a puzzle. The interconnectedness of Scripture can be seen in its literary flow: at first it seems like everything revolves around the Torah, only later seeing how everything ultimately orbits around Christ who alone fulfills the Torah. The covenantal/iterative flow (indicative-imperative-fulfillment triads) sheds light on the tension in Scripture where there is a persistent rejection of God. The death and resurrection of Christ provide a richer appreciation for how this tension is resolved only by Christ and the implications that this has on us. Thus, the Organism of Scripture helps us to see why Christ says that all of Scripture is about himself, particularly his death and resurrection.

In this chapter, we apply this approach to the Mosaic covenant, law, and tabernacle. The Mosaic covenant is pivotal since it explains the significance of God delivering Israel out of Egypt while foreshadowing the gospel of Christ. As a result, we not only appreciate the beauty of the rules and décor of God's dwelling place, but what they reveal about God, specifically his willingness to share his presence with humanity.

SETTING UP EXOD 19

Genesis 3 to Exod 18

There is much that transpired in the plot of Scripture from where we last left off (Gen 3) to where we are now (Exod 19). The approach in this book is crucial because it is here where there is a series of interesting narratives that can easily distract us from beholding the main points. The CREATOR-creature Distinction shows us that God is always the main character; the Problem of Sin reminds us that despite God's love and glory, his side characters refuse to trust and submit to him; and the Organism of Scripture helps us see the cohesion that underlies all these narratives and how they all point to Christ—especially his death and resurrection. Below is a table that not only summarizes the passages prior to Exod 19 but provides examples of applying this approach through the categories of the covenantal/iterative flow (indicatives, imperatives, and fulfillment):[1]

Passage	Indicatives	Imperatives	Fulfillment
Gen 4:1–16	God notices Cain's emotions, interacts with him, offers wisdom, and provides protection.	Cain to resist anger and submit to God's wisdom.	Cain is bitter toward God, ignores his wisdom, murders Abel, and leaves God's presence.
Gen 6–9	God notices the severity of sin and the utter wickedness of humanity but gives them another opportunity by setting aside Noah. This ensures that the promises from Gen 3:15–24 can be maintained.	Noah to follow the instructions for the ark.	Noah obeys the instructions, but sin and wickedness are still present in humanity; Noah falls into drunkenness.
Gen 11–12	Despite another chance, humanity rebels against God's command to multiply and subdue the earth by building a tower for their own sake. To maintain the promises of Gen 3:15–24, God sets aside Abram and gives more promises known as the "Abrahamic promises" (i.e., land, great nation, and the blessing dynamic; Gen 12:1–3).	Abram to leave his homeland and to go where God commands.	Abram trusts God by going to where he is led, but he distrusts God by fleeing to Egypt, lying, and risking the life of Sarai.
Gen 12–25	Generally, God's overall provision and trustworthiness over Abraham's life. God intimately walks with Abraham, reminding him of the trustworthiness of all his promises.	Abraham to trust God by waiting on the "Abrahamic promises" despite the impossibility of the situation.	Generally, Abraham trusts God, which is highlighted in his willingness to sacrifice the promised child, Isaac (Gen 22), but continues to have his moments of failure (Gen 20).

---

1. If unfamiliar with the general plot of Scripture, the following resource is very accessible and a great starting point: Bartholomew and Goheen, *Drama of Scripture*.

Gen 25–50	Generally, God's willingness to fulfill the Abrahamic promises and the initial promises of redemption (Gen 3:15–24) despite the immaturity and vice of all the side characters: Isaac, Rebekah, Esau, Jacob, Laban, Leah, Rachel, Reuben, Simeon, Levi, Judah, Tamar, Joseph, etc.	Generally, for everyone to trust God and not themselves, each other, or their circumstances.	Generally, there are very few instances where the side characters trust and submit to God. God nonetheless works out the plan to fulfill the Abrahamic promises (Gen 12:1–3) and the plan of redemption (Gen 3:15–24), but mostly despite the side characters. As a result, Genesis ends with a partial fulfillment of the Abrahamic promise: Abraham's descendants are a numerous nation, they possess the fertile land of Goshen, and God saved the known world through Joseph.
Exod 1–18	Generally, God multiplies Israel, protects them, remembers his covenant during their slavery, sets aside their redeemer (Moses), regards them as his firstborn son, performs ten miraculous signs, parts the Red Sea, appears to them in a pillar of cloud and fire, and provides gold, food, and water.	Generally, for everyone to trust God and not themselves, each other, or their circumstances.	Generally, everyone, including Moses, resists God's invitation to trust him. While Moses grows in his trust in God, Israel perpetually fails despite the indelible ways that God showcases his trustworthiness. Nonetheless, God continues to fulfill all his promises.

There are a few patterns that emerge from this table. First is that God maintains his promises not *because* of his people but *despite* them. Every good story needs a main character with whom we can relate. This character is usually the protagonist. The story also needs a villain who is compelling. This character is usually the antagonist. This approach helps us understand Scripture as intended, where God is not only the main character / protagonist, but the side characters are often the antagonists![2]

---

2. This is why God frequently regards his love as loyalty, often translated as "steadfast" (e.g., Gen 39:21; Exod 15:13, 20:6, 34:6; Deut 7:9; Ps 86:15). The primary gloss in *DCH* (Clines, *Dictionary of Classical Hebrew*) for the Hebrew *chesed* is "loyalty" (*DCH*, s.v. "חֶסֶד," 3:278–81). Similarly it is in *HALOT* (Koehler et al., *Hebrew and Aramaic Lexicon of the Old Testament*) as "joint obligation" or "faithfulness" (*HALOT*, s.v. "חֶסֶד," #3053).

Of course, this does not negate the few instances of trust expressed by the side characters. But these are few compared to the exorbitant number of failures. Moreover, even the most inspirational expressions of trust pale in comparison to who Christ is. Keeping an inventory of how the side characters fulfill the imperatives provides a much richer appreciation for the death and resurrection of Christ. In chapter 2, we learned that failed imperatives create the need to address *both* the consequences of sin and the requirements of God. Both of these are securely addressed by Christ. The failures of the side characters provide richer context for the death of Christ while the obedience of the side character provides richer context for his resurrection.

Notable Indicatives in Exod 1–18

As we did with Gen 1–3 (chapter 1), we must understand Exod 19–20 and 24 in the context of the indicative-imperative-fulfillment triad. Space only allows a list of a few of these indicatives:

1. A prominent reason for God delivering Israel out of Egypt is that Israel is God's firstborn son. God mentions this explicitly as a preface to the ten signs (Exod 4:21–23), and the tenth sign, the Passover, emphasizes the firstborn son (Exod 11–13). Since this section of Scripture begins and ends with the concept of firstborn son, it is an *inclusio*—a literary device to show the cohesion of a section of a text, usually to highlight the importance of the concept that frames that section. In short, the deliverance out of Egypt is God revealing himself as a Father to his firstborn son, Israel.[3]

2. Another reason for God delivering Israel is for "worship." This is first explained in Exod 3:12, but it was prophesied centuries prior to Abram (Gen 15:13), and it is mentioned throughout the exodus account (e.g., 3:12, 4:23, 7:16, 8:1). Although the word is usually translated as "serve," it has priestly connotations. It is the same Hebrew word, *'avad*, as what we saw earlier for Adam's priestly role (Gen 2:15; see also Num 3:7–8, 18:6). Later in the Mosaic covenant, it is even

---

So the independent CREATOR is more loyal to creatures for whom he has no need than creatures are to their independent CREATOR for whom they need everything!

3. Similarly, Childs, *Book of Exodus*, 102–3.

Christ as the True Israel (Exod 19-20, 24)

clearer that this kind of serving is not merely menial labor but priestly worship (Exod 19:5-6).

3. Related to 1 and 2, the reason for their deliverance is *not* comfort. There are much grander reasons for their deliverance. Israel failed to understand this, and therefore at the hint of any discomfort, they would turn against Moses and eventually God.

4. God's provision for Israel is extravagant. He not only demonstrates ten unforgettable signs that reveal unprecedented power, but he procures gold and other precious materials for them. This is first predicted to Abram (Gen 15:14; see also Exod 3:21-22, 11:2-3) and then mentioned as they are about to leave Egypt (Exod 12:35-36).

5. Throughout the deliverance, God patiently endures Israel's distrust and withholds his righteous judgment. Examples of their distrust are scattered throughout, usually in the form of accusing Moses and God of malice (e.g., Exod 3:10—4:13, 5:21-23, 6:9, 14:11-12, 15:24, 16:2-3, 17:3-4). The point of the exodus is not that Israel is an innocent victim who is lovable (e.g., Ezek 20:6-10) but that the love of God is steadfast.

These indicatives provide a necessary context to understand the Mosaic covenant, law, and tabernacle as intended. More specifically, when we see God as the main character throughout Scripture, we recognize striking similarities between passages that might otherwise seem disconnected. In both Gen 1-2 and Exod 1-18, God shares his presence with his people, reveals his character and promises, equips his people with everything they need to flourish, and designates his people with a sacred identity. The design is the same as Adam's: as Israel enjoys his presence, they can rule and be a blessing to the rest of the world (e.g., Gen 1:28-30, Isa 2:2-4, Mic 4:1-3). The indicatives are immense, yet the imperatives are simple: as God is inviting his people to live according to these indicatives, can they simply trust him?

INTRODUCING THE MOSAIC COVENANT

Whether it is the catchy line that there "ain't no mountain high enough" or the awe that overwhelms us when beholding a glorious view from the mountain top, we instinctively know the importance of mountains. It is therefore no surprise that the exodus account begins and ends on a mountain.[4] God initially calls Moses from the mountain and tells Moses to return to the same exact mountain with Israel (Exod 3:12). Accordingly, after Israel is rescued from Egypt, they are led to Mount Sinai (Exod 19:2). The word "mountain" is used sixteen times in Exod 19. When surveying other instances of mountains in Scripture, one of the fundamental principles consistently expressed is the CREATOR-creature Distinction. That God graciously condescends, reveals, and covenants with his people from on high is supposed to instill a sense of reverence and gratitude. God invites his people to ascend the mountain while he humbly deigns from his heavenly abode to share his presence.[5]

The Indicatives of God's Character and Promises

From the outset, God first reminds the people of his power and faithfulness:

> **You yourselves have seen what I did to the Egyptians**, and *how I bore you on eagles' wings and brought you to myself* (Exod 19:4).

So before God introduces the Mosaic covenant, law, or tabernacle—all of which might seem daunting—he reminds them of their shared history and experience:

a. God reminds them of his **power**: "**You yourselves have seen what I did to the Egyptians**"—this refers to all the miracles that he performed. With each passing sign and the parting of the Red Sea, Israel is progressively more amazed by the sheer power that God, their Father, possesses.

b. God expresses this in *poetic* language (*"how I bore you on eagles' wings"*) that exudes *intimacy* (*"and brought you to myself"*). God is not only powerful, but he is affectionate and loving—just like the perfect Father would be to his firstborn son.

In other words, God is pointing their attention to how trustworthy he has been so that they can trust him in the present and into the future. Thus,

---

4. This is an example of another inclusio.
5. This can also be easily distorted. During our recent trip to Banff, some of us were complaining about having to hike up a mountain (i.e., focusing too much on the imperatives), while those who had a better attitude focused more on the opportunity to hike up the mountain (i.e., appreciating the indicatives).

we see that even the Mosaic covenant, law, and tabernacle (like the rest of reality) are ultimately windows into God's character and promises. This is quite contrary to regarding the Mosaic covenant, law, and tabernacle as burdensome.

Before we move onto the next verses, it is helpful to be reminded of the CREATOR-creature Distinction. God has no need for anything outside himself. He does not need to explain his standards, demands, or requirements to humanity. Nor does he need to appeal to his trustworthiness with poetic and affectionate language. He can simply assert what he desires and wills. This authoritative approach, however, is not how God establishes the Mosaic covenant (nor how he started his relationship with humanity in Gen 1–3). Seeing these passages (and eventually all of reality) in the context of the CREATOR-creature Distinction sheds light on so many glorious aspects of God that we would otherwise overlook.

Next, God reveals his promises:

> Now therefore, if you will indeed obey my voice and keep my covenant, you shall be my treasured possession among all peoples, for all the earth is mine; and you shall be to me a kingdom of priests and a holy nation. (Exod 19:5–6)

One of the purposes of delivering Israel from Egypt is for them to receive a new identity. Israel is to forsake their old identity as slaves and embrace their new identity as God's "treasured possession, . . . a kingdom of priests and a holy nation." This is remarkable since God is sovereign of "all the earth." There are certainly mightier peoples. Yet God has chosen Israel because he is true to his promises (Gen 12:1–3; see also 3:15).

The Indicative of God Sharing His Presence

As mentioned throughout this book, an adequate summary of Scripture is God's willingness to share his presence with his people. This is precisely what occurs before God establishes the Mosaic covenant. There is, however, a problem. On the one hand, God is perfect in righteousness. Even sinless angels cannot dare to look upon his holiness (e.g., Isa 6:2). On the other hand, all of humanity since Gen 3, including Israel, is sinful. So although God is willing to regard Israel as his firstborn son, his treasured possession, a kingdom of priests, and a holy nation, how can a sinful people be recipients of God's holy presence?

Like us, Israel does not fully grasp the eternal barrier that is caused by the depths of their sin and the heights of God's righteousness. There is a sense of naivete in how they are approaching their relationship with God, thinking that "all that the Lord has spoken we will do" (Exod 19:8; cf. 19:17). God therefore provides Israel a glimpse of the consequences of this barrier as he descends from his heavenly abode to Mount Sinai in a thick cloud (Exod 19:9). God further instructs Moses to consecrate the people by washing their garments and avoiding sexual activity, and to inform them *not* to ascend the mountain lest they die (Exod 19:10–15). At first blush, these instructions might seem unkind, but, like all of God's instructions, they are given to benefit Israel—literally to save their lives!

As God lowers himself onto the mountain, thunder, lightning, smoke, and quaking erupt (Exod 19:16–19). Essentially the holy Creator who is full of glory is breaking into the earthly realm that has been corrupted by sin. The people, therefore, tremble in great fear (Exod 19:16) as their very lives are jeopardized (Exod 19:21–24). They verbalize their appropriate fear when they beseech Moses, "You speak to us, and we will listen; but do not let God speak to us, lest we die" (Exod 20:19). If the people were earlier overconfident about being in God's presence by taking "their stand at the foot of the mountain" (Exod 19:17), then this experience has shaken that confidence as they are now content with being "far off" (Exod 20:21). We see later that God provides the sacrificial laws so that the people can eventually approach him with confidence.

God orchestrates this frightening experience so that Israel can have a better sense of God's majesty and their sin. As the covenant is being established, they have a better grasp that God is full of power and that his presence should not be taken for granted.

An important point that we typically overlook despite Scripture making it emphatically clear is that the deliverance from Egypt and gracing Israel with his presence happen *before* the covenant is established and the law is revealed.[6] In other words, God performs miracles for his people and is with them before he ever expects anything from them. This is yet another example of how the imperatives must flow inextricably from the indicatives. More importantly, this is the same flow of the gospel of Christ: Christ first rescues us from sin and permanently dwells in us through the Holy

---

6. Here we see the dynamic of the Creator-creature Distinction: God reveals (deliverance from Egypt), condescends (shares his presence), and covenants (Mosaic covenant).

Spirit (indicatives) so that we can live according to God's righteousness (imperative), which has been imputed to us and is what we will inevitably embody (fulfillment).

THE LAW

Only after God delivers Israel from Egypt and shares his presence with them does God reveal the law to Israel in the context of a covenant. The centerpiece of the law is the Ten Commandments (Exod 20:1–17). The translation to "laws" or "commandments," however, is imprecise. The original Hebrew (*davar*) and the later Greek translations (*logos* and *rhēma*) are more accurately translated as "words" (e.g., Exod 20:1, 24:3–4), and the Hebrew word *torah* primarily means "instruction" or "teaching" (Exod 24:12).[7] Accordingly, the primary purpose of the law is not mindless obedience or blind action. Instead, the purpose of "words" or "teachings" is reflection.[8] Israel is invited to reflect upon these important teachings or words—all of which are windows into God's character and promises.[9]

God introduces the ten words the same way he introduces the covenant (Exod 19:4–6), by highlighting his character and promises. Notice the opening words:

> *I am the* LORD *your God*, who **brought you out of the land of Egypt, out of the house of slavery.** (Exod 20:2)

The indicative-imperative-fulfillment pattern persists. Before disclosing the commandments (or "words"), he reminds the people of who he is (character) and what he has done (promises). "*I am the* LORD *your God*" is a phrase

---

7. Also a common name for the Ten Commandments is the Decalogue, which is Greek for ten (*deka*) words (*logos*). Similarly, see Meyers, *Exodus*, 163.

8. This is especially apparent when understanding laws in the ancient Near East (e.g., Ur-Namma, Hammurabi, etc.). With a greater understanding of the cultural context, it becomes clear how relational and personal God is in the Torah. For instance, there is no other evidence in the ancient Near East where a deity addresses an entire group of people (usually addressed only to kings or certain people); in the Torah, God commonly uses the first-person pronoun ("I") while addressing Israel with the second-person pronoun ("you"), which is rare (usually in the third-person, "he"); and the Ten Words are technically not laws but are more apodictic (not casuistic), so they foster reflection more than action. For more, see Strawn, *Bible and Law*.

9. Childs likewise writes, "The commandments are tied inextricably to God's revelation at Sinai. . . . They reflected the essential character of God himself." *Book of Exodus*, 397.

that refers to God's character. Not only does it remind the people that he is God (i.e., the Creator-creature Distinction) but that he is *their* God (i.e., he has been faithful to them). The next line, "**brought you out of the land of Egypt, out of the house of slavery**," is a reminder of all that God performed and Israel witnessed—that is, every miracle performed further sears into their hearts the omnipotence and sovereignty of God so that they do not forget, though he knows that they will. This phrase in bold also asserts that he is true to his promises. God fulfills a promise that is humanly impossible by delivering Israel out of Egypt. If he can fulfill this promise, then certainly his promises are as trustworthy as his character.

It is only after God establishes the foundation of these indicatives that we have the footing to reflect upon the imperatives. Otherwise, we are tempted to distort these laws, essentially repeating Gen 3:1–6 (see also Rom 1:18–32). For instance, our instinct is to view the laws from a human-centered standpoint: How do they benefit me? Am I guilty of any of them? How might this provide societal stability? If this is our starting point, then it will inevitably lead to self-righteousness, excessive introspection, an unhealthy sense of burden, or other side effects. While there are certainly favorable implications of following God's law, it is first a window into who he is. We must therefore first reflect upon what this law says about God's character and promises.

Let us take the eighth commandment as an example: "You shall not steal" (Exod 20:15). The following diagram and table provide steps to reflect upon this teaching or word as intended:

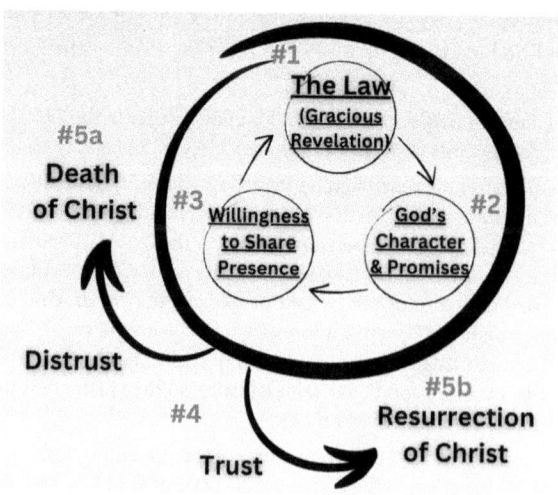

Christ as the True Israel (Exod 19–20, 24)

#1	**God's Law:** Remember that God has no need for humanity, so all his revelation, including his laws, is an expression of grace and is for the benefit of humanity. Our reflection upon any law should therefore begin with a sense of gratitude and reverence.	**Indicative**
#2	**God's Character and Promises:** Often when we think of a law, our immediate focus is on ourselves or how burdensome the law is. This is essentially what happened in Adam and Eve in Gen 3 and plays out in countless ways in Scripture and in our own lives. The primary purpose of this law is to reveal God's character and promises. Before considering how we must apply the law, we must be disciplined by first pondering what this law says about God's character and promises. One of the immediate aspects that should stand out for Israel at this point in their history is that there is no need to steal because God is a gracious provider. From the opening chapters of Genesis, God abundantly provides for humanity, even after their rebellion. In his journeys with Abraham, God provided for all his needs, including promises that were inconceivable. In the lives of the patriarchs, God proved to be generous—whether it was blessing Isaac with a wife and the promised child or prospering the life of Jacob. God's bountiful provisions continue in the life of Joseph, multiplying Israel, the deliverance out of Egypt, and the miraculous supply of food and water. In virtually every chapter of Scripture thus far—from Gen 1 to Exod 18—God fulfills the needs of his people. This is why the Decalogue begins with "I am the LORD your God, who brought you out of the land of Egypt, out of the house of slavery" (Exod 20:2)—if God provided deliverance from Egypt, then certainly he is Israel's provider whom they can trust. "You shall not steal" is less an onerous burden than it is a gracious reminder of God's character and promises. Israel can trust in their God and do not need to take matters into their own hands. Rather than experiencing the guilt of stealing or putting on pressure to provide for themselves, they can find peace and freedom in yielding to their trustworthy provider.	**Indicative**

#3	**God's Presence:**	
	God's character and promises culminate in his willingness to share his presence with us. We enjoy his presence by submitting to his loving reign over us as we trust in his law. Hence, our motivation to obey his word should be more about his presence and reign over us rather than our sense of guilt, obligation, self-righteousness, or anything that is not relational with God.	**Indicative**
	"You shall not steal" is therefore less a commandment to follow blindly and more an invitation to live according to who God is. As Israel submits to and trusts in this teaching, they experience God's joyful reign and life-giving presence in this aspect of their life.	
#4	**God's Invitation:**	
	God's people are invited to live according to his character and promises so that they can enjoy his presence in all aspects of life. His people are therefore called to trust and submit to his laws. By not trusting and rejecting his laws, they are rebelling against his gracious revelation and depriving themselves of true life.	**Imperative**
	Because of Israel's sinful nature, they cannot keep God's law. As much as there are ample examples of God's faithfulness to provide for his people, there are examples of his people's failure to trust, and their resort to stealing. Rather than trusting in God's prophecy, Jacob steals both the birthright and the blessing of his twin, Esau (Gen 25:29–34; 27). In the face of God's faithful provision, Rachel steals the idol from her father's household (Gen 31:19). These examples are not just about stealing, as if it is merely a vice or a crime against humans. Rather, stealing is fundamentally relational—defiance against the character and promises of God. Israel, of course, is a spiritual mirror to us, so their inability to keep this commandment is a reflection of our own failure. Why does such a holy God who is perfect in righteousness tolerate such egregious sins of his people?	
#5	**Christ's Fulfillment:**	
	God's people have not fulfilled the law; instead they have repeatedly violated it. Christ fulfills the law in two ways:	**Fulfillment**
	a. Christ fulfills the *consequences* of breaking the law on behalf of his people through his death. Thus, the failure of his people is tolerated by God.	
	b. Christ fulfills the *requirements* of following the law by not stealing and trusting in God's provision. This righteousness is shared with his people through his resurrection: the Father declares his people to be righteous in Christ and the Spirit conforms his people to embody the righteousness of Christ.	

Although these steps might seem simple, they are rarely applied. When they are followed, the results are transformative since we organically and

Christ as the True Israel (Exod 19–20, 24)

meaningfully see the death and resurrection of Christ. With these steps, we can now apply them to other biblical laws so that we can understand them as intended.[10]

RATIFYING THE MOSAIC COVENANT

After revealing the Ten Commandments (Exod 20:1–17), God reveals additional laws known as the book of the covenant (Exod 21–23) before ratifying the Mosaic covenant (Exod 24). It is in this ratification process that God reveals two things that are profoundly unexpected and significant.

God's Presence with Sinful People Requires Sacrifice

God invites Moses, Aaron, Nadab and Abihu, and the seventy elders to draw near, but only Moses is permitted to the summit of the mountain

---

10. Here are two other examples:

(a) In the second commandment where Israel is not to make a carved image, God refers to his character (he is a "jealous God") and his promise (he will visit their iniquity) (Exod 20:4–6). These aspects of God's character and promises might appear to be intimidating or unloving, similar to how Adam and Eve perceived God's commandments in Gen 3. However, it is once again important to be reminded of the Creator-creature Distinction. God has no need for humanity. Everything that God has revealed, which includes the Mosaic covenant and the law, is an expression of his gracious condescension. Humanity is not so valuable that it warrants God's attention, let alone his jealousy. Moreover, while human jealousy is often inappropriate, jealousy can be a fitting response. At its essence, jealousy is the righteous reaction when something precious that belongs to you is improperly given to someone else (e.g., in a marriage). Everything, including all our worship and allegiance, rightfully belongs to God, so his jealousy is both an expression of his love and righteousness. Additionally, God knows that the party that suffers from idolatry are the idolaters. One of the consequences of idolatry is that humanity is preposterously severing itself from the only source of life. Hence this commandment that appears harsh is for the benefit of Israel. As parents or teachers, strong warnings at times are not only necessary but loving. In the same way, "jealousy" in this context is best understood as God's love, which is why the commandment ends with "steadfast love" (Exod 20:6).

(b) Later, in what scholars consider the book of the covenant (Exod 21–23), God warns Israel of mistreating the sojourner and exacting interest from the poor (Exod 22:21–27). God explains the rationale underlying each of these laws by appealing to his own character and promise. This simple point is a strong corrective to the way we typically view laws (e.g., almost exclusively in a human-centered way). It is because God is compassionate that Israel must not wrong the sojourner—again, the point of Exod 22:24 is not that God is harsh but that he cares for the sojourner, widow, the fatherless, and the poor (Exod 22:22–23, 27).

(Exod 24:1–2). Before they scale the mountain, something seemingly unnecessary occurs: Moses builds an altar, makes sacrifices, and throws blood on the altar and the people (Exod 24:4–8). With the questions raised earlier about the eternal barrier between God's righteousness and Israel's sinfulness, these actions make perfect sense.

A sacrifice is necessary to bridge this eternal barrier so that a holy God can fellowship with a sinful people. Earlier, the people only consecrated themselves through water and abstinence (Exod 19:10–15), but here there is blood. This follows the logic that is later outlined in Leviticus (the next book of the Bible). In order to approach God's presence in the tabernacle, the people must first consecrate themselves—usually involving water (Lev 11–15). Once this has been done, the people are then able to offer sacrifices so that they can enjoy communion with God (Lev 1–7).

Although the sacrificial law is not given until Leviticus, its importance has already been revealed several times. As we saw in the first chapter, an animal needed to be sacrificed for Adam and Eve to cover their nakedness (Gen 3:21). The details of Gen 3 show that this covering is not to warm them or prevent sickness. The covering is to address the shame and guilt that were caused by their sin so that some kind of a relationship with the holy God can be maintained (Gen 3:10). This pivotal role of sacrifice underlies Noah's account (Gen 6:5–7, 8:20–22): even after the flood, humanity still remains in its hopeless sin ("for the intention of man's heart is evil from his youth"—Gen 8:21; cf. 6:5–7). Thus, there should be nothing but God's righteous wrath upon them. Nevertheless, God withholds his wrath and instead makes a promise known as the Noahic covenant (Gen 8:21—9:17). Why? Because of Noah's sacrifice (Gen 8:20–21). In short, God provides sacrifice to address sin so that sinners can commune with God. If animal sacrifice is what enabled Adam/Eve and Noah to commune with God, then what difference will Moses's sacrifice make in this passage?

God's Presence as a Glimpse of a Heavenly Reality

After the sacrifice, Moses and the others climb the mountain, and God reveals the first unexpected thing: "They saw the God of Israel" (Exod 24:10). This is an expression of the CREATOR-creature Distinction:

> There was under his feet as it were a pavement of sapphire stone, like the very heaven for clearness. (Exod 24:10)

Christ as the True Israel (Exod 19–20, 24)

In other words, they are looking up to God, so they see the bottom of his feet. The heavenly reality that we see in other portions of Scripture depicts God sitting upon his throne which is above everything else (e.g., Ps 99:1, Isa 6:1, Rev 4:2).

It is not just God's feet that they see but "a pavement of sapphire stone, like the very heaven for clearness" (Exod 24:10). This strange image is described in Gen 1 and Ezek 1. In Genesis, God creates a separation between the heavenly and earthly realms on the second day (Gen 1:6–8). God achieves this separation by creating an expanse whose color is blue. In the ancient Near East, the sky is a blue boundary or border (often called an expanse or firmament) that separates the waters of above (heavenly realm) from waters below (earthly realm). It is only during this second day of creation that God does not make the comment that "it was good."

Ezekiel witnesses something similar in his own vision of God's heavenly abode (Ezek 1:4–28). Initially Ezekiel sees the living creatures who have wings (Ezek 1:4–25). We typically get sidetracked by the intrigue of these creatures rather than beholding the main point of this passage. In this vision, Ezekiel sees "above" the living creatures: something like an "expanse, shining like awe-inspiring crystal" and a "throne" that is "sapphire" (Ezek 1:22, 26). The word "sapphire" is significant because this is the only other time in Scripture that this word, *safir*, is used to describe something other than the priestly ephod.

Taking all these passages together, Moses and Ezekiel are seeing God's heavenly abode, which is represented by his throne. Thus, they each see the bottom of God's feet. What separates God's heavenly abode from their earthly abode is something that looks like an expanse/pavement that is sapphire/blue. In short, God is offering a glimpse of a heavenly reality.

God's Presence as Intimate Communion

As Moses and others behold this heavenly reality, the second unexpected thing occurs:

> And he did not **lay his hand** on the chief men of the people of Israel; *they beheld God, and ate and drank.* (Exod 24:11)

God is offering not only a glimpse of heaven but intimate communion. This verse by itself might not seem significant without the background of the traumatic experience of Exod 19–20. Thus, it is important to return to the questions raised earlier: How can a holy God share his presence with sinful people? And what difference does Moses's sacrifice make? Let's explore how this verse is written and its context to appreciate how God answers these questions.

The phrase "**lay his hand**" is a Hebrew idiom that often conveys something threatening (e.g., Exod 22:10, 12; 37:22).[11] In this context, Israel would have associated this with how God uses it for himself when striking Egypt with signs (Exod 3:20, 9:15). The idea is that Moses and others should be threatened by God like the earlier experience (Exod 19–20), but God chooses not to strike them. Instead, they "beheld God, and ate and drank," which is an expression of intimacy.[12] What causes the drastic shift from being endangered by God's holiness to enjoying communion with God? It is Moses's sacrifice (Exod 24:4–8). As mentioned above, the importance of sacrifice has been adumbrated several times already and is ultimately a precursor to the death of Christ:

Passage	Sacrifice	God's Grace
Gen 3:10, 21	God kills animals to procure garments for Adam and Eve	God covers Adam and Eve's shame so that a relationship can still be maintained.
Gen 6:5–7, 8:20–22	Noah's sacrifice after the flood	God makes a promise (the Noahic covenant) rather than sending another calamity so that a relationship can still be maintained.
Exod 19–20, 24	Moses's sacrifice before approaching God's presence	The people can enjoy a glimpse of heaven and intimate fellowship with God rather than their lives being threatened by his holiness.
Leviticus	A system of sacrificial laws	The people receive perpetual forgiveness of sin in an organized and sustainable way so that they can regularly enjoy God's presence.

---

11. There are a few exceptions, e.g., Gen 48:14.

12. In the words of Childs, "The effect of the whole description is one of awe-inspiring majesty leading far beyond the human imagination, but one which recedes from all concrete particulars. The description turns to describe, as if in amazement, the fact that the elders could behold God and still live. . . . But in the light of God's complete otherness, the all-encompassing focus of the chapter falls on God's mercy and gracious condescension. It is the theme which lies at the heart of the witness of the Sinai covenant." *Book of Exodus*, 507–8.

| New Testament | The Father offers his own Son for his enemies | The people receive eternal forgiveness for all sins—past, present, and future—because of the efficacy of divine and perfectly righteous blood. |

Another Example of the Narrative Diagram

Before commenting on the significance of the tabernacle, here is an example of applying the narrative diagram for Exod 24:

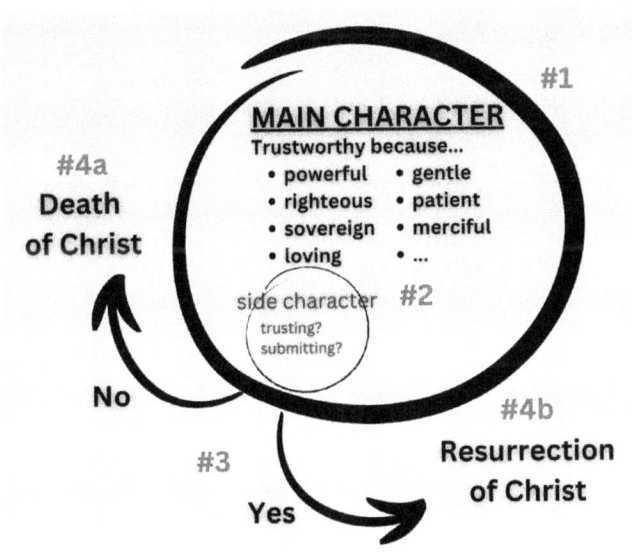

#1	The Trustworthiness of the Main Character:	
	God is the one who delivered Israel out of Egypt miraculously in order to initiate the Mosaic covenant; he is the one who shares his presence by inviting Moses and others up the mountain; God specifies how the people can approach him so that they do not perish from his holiness; and God accepts the sacrifice.	Indicative
#2	God's Invitation:	
	In the light of the ample reasons for the side characters to trust God (#1), God is inviting them to trust in him—his character and promises. The fundamental question concerning the side characters is whether they trust in God. In this passage, God explicitly invites them to draw near (Exod 24:1–2).	Imperative

#3	**Israel's Trust:** In this passage, the side characters trust and obey God's instructions. This is mostly influenced by the faithfulness of Moses, who functions as the mediator between God and Israel. He rightly offers a sacrifice to approach God's holiness. As a result, rather than God "laying his hand" on the people, God extends mercy by allowing them to have intimate fellowship with him.	**Fulfillment**
#4	**Christ's Fulfillment:** How does this passage enrich our appreciation for the death and resurrection of Christ? In what ways does this passage provide more context to the death and resurrection of Christ? Christ fulfills the imperative in two ways: a. Christ fulfills the *consequences* of failing the imperative on behalf of his people through his death. Thus, the failure of his people is tolerated by God. b. Christ fulfills the *requirements* of following the imperative by perfectly trusting and obeying God. The trust from his people foreshadows the perfect righteousness of Christ. This righteousness is shared with his people through his resurrection: the Father declares his people to be righteous in Christ and the Spirit conforms his people to embody the righteousness of Christ. #4b is accented in this example. As much as Moses is faithful in this passage, it is limited and merely foreshadows the perfect faithfulness of Christ. In chapter 5, we will see that, unlike Moses, Christ is able to take anyone to the summit of the mountain. Christ is the superior mediator who does not grant his people temporary access to God's presence on Mount Sinai, but eternal access to the heavenly places. Christ does not merely give his people a view from below the throne, but seats them with himself at the right hand of the Father. All this is possible because his death provides the forgiveness that his people need (so #4a is still relevant), and his people can share his righteousness that they need through the resurrection.	**Fulfillment**

THE TABERNACLE

The tabernacle has a terrible reputation that is unwarranted. It is often perceived as laborious or even barbaric. Thus, God first establishes many indicatives that reveal his character and promises—namely, his willingness to share his presence with his people—before revealing details about the tabernacle. Regrettably, however, we overlook these indicatives and take

Christ as the True Israel (Exod 19–20, 24)

the imperatives out of context (just like Gen 3:1–6). Now that some of the major indicatives have been highlighted, we are now able to see how the imperatives pertaining to the tabernacle are a glorious invitation. In short, the tabernacle is God's gracious provision for his people to enjoy his presence in a sustainable manner—offering not only a glimpse of what humanity forfeited in the garden of Eden, but the heavenly reality that is secured for us in Christ.[13]

The gift of the tabernacle means that God's presence is not confined to a mountain, because the tabernacle becomes a portable environment where this communion can be maintained. Exodus 25–40 are essentially the instructions on how to build the tabernacle, while the entire book of Leviticus is essentially the instructions on how to operate the tabernacle. Leviticus is the poster child for perceiving God as impersonal or demanding because it is full of laws for purification and sacrifice. But the context established by this approach toward Scripture affords an accurate understanding of Leviticus: the laws for purification and sacrifice are not burdensome but are intended to avoid the trauma that Israel experienced (Exod 19–20) so that they can be in God's holy presence despite their sinfulness. The consecration and sacrifice that took place in the ratification of the covenant (Exod 19:10–15, 24:4–8) are systematized in Leviticus. Therefore, instead of Israel being endangered by God's holiness, they are routinely invited into a heavenly reality as they bask in intimate communion with God.

As far as the construction of the tabernacle (Exod 25–40), limitations of this book permit only a few observations.

The Tabernacle as Invitation Not Exclusion

First is the threefold layout of the tabernacle as depicted in the diagram below:

---

13. Another way of expressing this paragraph is to see the flow of the Creator-creature Distinction, the Problem of Sin, and the Organism of Scripture (and the indicative-imperative-fulfillment triad). God graciously reveals and condescends to his people even though his people distort, suppress, and reject this revelation. Only Christ is the one who enables his people to recognize and live according to this revelation as intended.

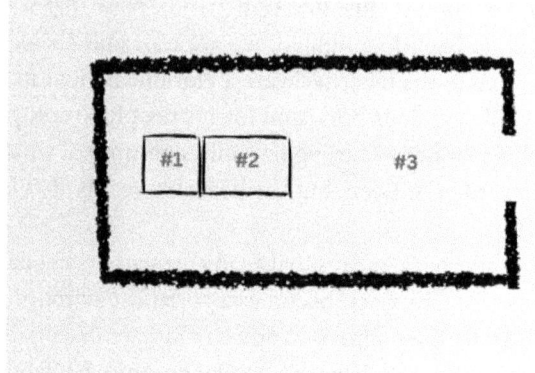

As one enters the tabernacle from the east, they enter into the courtyard (#3). Only priests are allowed in the Holy Places (#1 and 2): the Holy Place (#2) is for any priest while the Most Holy Place (#1) is only for the high priest to enter yearly (on Yom Kippur or the Day of Atonement). The reason why there are three areas in the tabernacle is to convey the holiness of God. As we saw in how God creates, there is a need for separation—not ultimately to exclude, but first to express God's holiness and second to indicate God's willingness to provide a way for people to access his holiness. In short, the boundaries that "exclude" are revealed to show how *inclusive* God is and how we should not take God's invitation for granted.

The tabernacle conveys this threefold layout horizontally. This same layout is present in Israel's experience on Mount Sinai, but vertically (Exod 19–24):[14]

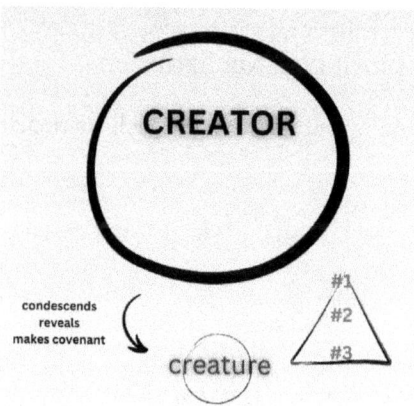

---

14. So Milgrom, *Leviticus 1–16*, 142–43.

So the Most Holy Place corresponds with the summit of the mountain, allowing only a single individual to access (#1); the Holy Place with the top of the mountain, for a select group (#2); and the courtyard with the base of the mountain, for all the people (#3).

The Tabernacle as Heavenly

The reason why the construction of the tabernacle is so detailed is that it reflects a heavenly reality. Thus, the proper way of understanding the specified dimensions of the tabernacle (Exod 25–40) is not in emphasizing how demanding or picky God is but that he is willing to allow sinners to enjoy something heavenly. This is hinted in the following verses where God instructs Moses that these details are copies of a heavenly reality, and later clarified in the New Testament:

> Exactly as I show you concerning *the pattern of the tabernacle*, and of all its furniture, so you shall make it. (Exod 25:9; see also 25:40, 26:3)

> Our fathers had the tent of witness in the wilderness, just as he who spoke to Moses directed him to make it, according to *the pattern* that he had seen. (Acts 7:44)

> They serve **a copy and shadow of the heavenly things**. For when Moses was about to erect the tent, he was instructed by God, saying, "See that you make everything according to *the pattern* that was shown you on the mountain." (Heb 8:5; see also 9:23, 10:1)

Every time God's people enter into the tabernacle, it is not to execute inconvenient rituals of purification or sacrifice—rather, they are ushered into a heavenly reality to commune with the independent CREATOR!

The Tabernacle Looking Back and Forward

By now there is a recurring pattern. God's revelation points backward and forward. For instance, Israel's deliverance from Egypt has striking similarities with the creation account, but the deliverance is also a preview of the gospel. These patterns become apparent when we are trained to see Scripture as intended through this threefold approach. By consistently recognizing that God is the main character, a beautiful constancy emerges, though it never gets old since it is expressed in diverse and suspenseful ways. After all, God is *the* storyteller telling us *the* story about himself.

The tabernacle is another example of this pattern. The tabernacle is an opportunity to experience the essence of both the garden of Eden of the past and the new creation of the future. This reality is expressed through a number of details. God places cherubim to guard the *east* of the garden of Eden (Gen 3:24). In Scripture, angelic figures are positioned to signal various boundaries so that God's holiness can be expressed. This is why the two curtains within the tabernacle are decorated with cherubim. The first curtain is at the entrance of the tabernacle, which is on the *east* (Exod 26:1). Thus, the layout of the tabernacle mirrors that of the garden of Eden. The second curtain, which is decorated with cherubim, is in between the Holy Place and the Most Holy Place, which is also decorated with cherubim (Exod 26:31). Later in the vision of the new creation, we see angels surrounding God's presence (e.g., Rev 21:12).

Moreover, the Most Holy Place contains the ark of the covenant. The ark of the covenant is richly symbolic. At the top of the ark is the central mercy seat, which is consistently described as being *above* (Exod 25:21, 22; see also Heb 9:5). The mercy seat is flanked by two cherubim. The idea is that God's heavenly throne is above everything and is surrounded by angels to protect other creatures from God's holiness. This aligns with the CREATOR-creature Distinction, the images that both Moses and Ezekiel saw (Exod 24:11, Ezek 1:22–26), and the rationale of cherubim being positioned to guard the garden of Eden and engraved in the curtains of the tabernacle. Thus, in other accounts of this heavenly reality, we see that angelic creatures surround God's throne (e.g., Ps 99, Isa 6, Rev 4). So all the rituals pertaining to the tabernacle are reminders of the centrality of the ark of the covenant. The mercy seat symbolizes that they are invited to God's heavenly throne even though they should not be permitted. Nevertheless, God draws sinners, enabling them to pass through each layer of holiness that is guarded by cherubim, because God's mercy ultimately prevails *above* their sin.

There are many other parallels between the tabernacle, the garden of Eden, and the new creation (e.g., plants, lampstand, gold, water, etc.). The point in all these parallels is that the tabernacle is another opportunity for people to enjoy God's presence as they did in the garden of Eden and will do eternally in the new creation.

Christ as the True Israel (Exod 19–20, 24)

FULFILLING THE MOSAIC COVENANT

The Imperative and Failed Fulfillment

In summary, we have seen that the way God introduces the Mosaic covenant, law, and tabernacle are laden with indicatives. Although the Mosaic covenant is an expression of God's grace, Israel does not respond accordingly. God invites Israel to live according to these indicatives (imperative), but as soon as Israel has the opportunity to respond to the covenant, they breach it by creating and worshiping a golden calf (Exod 32–34—failed fulfillment). This can be seen more clearly when applying the narrative diagram:

#1	**The Trustworthiness of the Main Character:** God has proven his trustworthiness by hearing Israel's cry and remembering the covenant that he has made to the patriarchs; he has demonstrated his power through the ten signs and the parting of the Red Sea; he has blessed Israel with gold; and he has provided them with water, manna, and quail. That he is making a covenant with Israel is an expression of unthinkable grace and love.	Indicative
#2	**God's Invitation:** In the light of the ample reasons for Israel to trust God (#1), God is inviting Israel to trust in him—his character and promises. The most fundamental question concerning the side character, Israel, is whether they trust God.	Imperative
#3	**Israel's Distrust:** Despite #1 and 2, Israel immediately and repeatedly fails. At their first chance, they attribute the deliverance from Egypt to the golden calf that they themselves make with the gold that God provided (Exod 32–24); Israel forsakes their holy identity by being led astray to idolatry by the Canaanites; and throughout Israel's history, they consistently violate all the stipulations of the Mosaic covenant.	Fulfillment

#4	**Christ's Fulfillment:** How does this passage enrich our appreciation for the death and resurrection of Christ? In what ways does this passage provide more context to the death and resurrection of Christ? Christ fulfills the imperative in two ways: a. Christ fulfills the *consequences* of failing the imperative on behalf of his people through his death. Thus, the failure of his people is tolerated by God. b. Christ fulfills the *requirements* of following the imperative by perfectly trusting and obeying God. The trust from his people foreshadows the perfect righteousness that Christ fulfills. This righteousness is shared with his people through his resurrection: the Father declares his people to be righteous in Christ and the Spirit conforms his people to embody the righteousness of Christ #4a is accented in this example: the sins of idolatry from his people are paid through his death. However, #4b is also relevant. Where Israel fell into idolatry (#4a), Christ fulfills the requirement of worshiping only God with all his heart, mind, and strength (#4b). This righteousness is shared with his people through his resurrection.	**Fulfillment**

The golden calf fiasco (Exod 32–34) is not an isolated failure. Scripture shows that Israel perpetually forsakes their identity as a "treasured possession," "kingdom of priests," and "holy nation" by falling into idolatry. As early as the book of Judges, Israel becomes even more detestable than the Canaanites. Yet, God's faithfulness endures. He graciously provides additional covenants and opportunities for Israel to live as God's firstborn son. Finally, the Old Testament ends with the promise of a new covenant where he will address the underlying Problem of Sin. God will give them "a new heart, and a new spirit" (Ezek 36:26; see also Jer 31:31–34), which of course is by the death and resurrection of Christ.

The Fulfillment of Christ

This new covenant is ultimately fulfilled by Christ. In chapter 6, we will explore further, but for now let us reflect upon what Peter writes:

> But you are a chosen race, a royal priesthood, a holy nation, a people for his own possession, that you may proclaim the excellencies

of him who called you out of darkness into his marvelous light. (1 Pet 2:9)

Peter intentionally uses the same diction of "a chosen race, royal priesthood, a holy nation, a people for his own possession" to evoke what God promised in Exod 19:5–6 ("a treasured possession among all peoples, for all the earth is mine; and you shall be to me a kingdom of priests and a holy nation"). The difference is that in Exod 19, Israel "shall" be these things whereas from Peter's vantage point, they already "are" these things. What is the key factor in this difference? Once again, the death and resurrection of Christ.

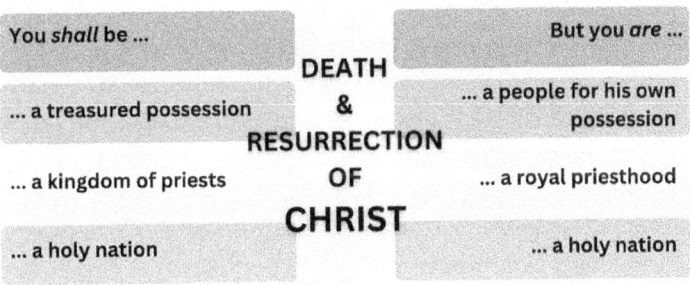

So the Mosaic covenant should evoke a sense of gratitude for God's merciful condescension, revelation, and commitment toward Israel. There is also a sense of anticipation and hope that Israel can shed its identity as a slave and live as God's firstborn son. They are to be the beneficiaries of God's presence and the revelation of his character and promises, enabling them to be the fulfillment of the promises to Abraham and Adam. But the full story showcases something far more glorious: Christ is the True Israel, and only by his death and resurrection, we are declared to be his treasured possession, royal priesthood, and holy nation.

SUMMARY

As Airbnb rules and décor disclose much about the landlord, we see that the law and the tabernacle reveal much about God's character and promises. This chapter applied the threefold approach to Scripture so that we can understand the essence of the Mosaic covenant, law, and tabernacle. These are crucial to recognize the purpose of Israel's deliverance and how it is a template for the gospel of Christ.

The Mosaic covenant is a beautiful example of the Creator-creature Distinction. As God condescends to Mount Sinai, he reveals to his people his character and promises through the law. The law is not primarily about what they are to do but who God is. For instance, God's people are not to lie because God speaks only in truth and all his promises are trustworthy. Part of these promises is that Israel is bestowed with a new identity. No longer are they slaves of Egypt but God's firstborn son and treasured possession. Ultimately, God blesses the people with the tabernacle where they can delight in his holy presence despite their sin.

Much like Adam and Eve, Israel neglects these indicatives and misunderstands the Mosaic covenant. The Problem of Sin means that Israel twists God's precious revelation by making it about something else. They think that their deliverance is for their own comfort, and therefore the Mosaic covenant is often considered a nuisance.

Nonetheless, the Organism of Scripture shows that every road of the Old Testament—whether it is the garden of Eden, the deliverance from Egypt, or the tabernacle—not only leads to, but is grounded, saturated, and culminating in Christ alone.[15] While Israel fails irreverently, Christ fulfills by absorbing the consequences of his people's failures and actively accomplishing the requirements of God on behalf of his people.

When these biblical principles sink into our hearts, we recognize that our deliverance from sin mirrors Israel's deliverance from Egypt. The purpose of our deliverance is the same: to relish continually in God's character, promises, and presence; to gain a new identity; to live in worship and holiness; and to be a light for others. Sadly, we reduce the gospel of Christ as merely the forgiveness of sins and therefore a license to live how ever we please. Like Israel, we often disregard God's law as unnecessary or cumbersome. But like Israel, our only hope has always been in Christ. Thus, every road of life—whether our successes or failures, our promotions or layoffs,

---

15. So Bavinck writes, "And since Christ was the real content of the Old Testament revelation (John 5:39; 1 Peter 1:11; and Rev. 19:10), He is in the dispensation of the new covenant also its capstone and crown. He is the fulfillment of the law, of all righteousness (Matt. 3:15 and 5:17), of all promises, which in Him are yea and amen (2 Cor. 1:20), of the new covenant which is now established in His blood (Matt. 26:28). The people of Israel itself, with all its history, its offices and institutions, its temple and its altar, its sacrifices and ceremonies, its prophecy, psalmody, and wisdom teaching, achieves its goal and purpose in Him." *Our Reasonable Faith*, 94.

CHRIST AS THE TRUE ISRAEL (EXOD 19–20, 24)

our joy or grief—not only leads to, but is grounded, saturated, and culminating in Christ alone.

QUESTIONS FOR REFLECTION AND PRAYER

a. Review the table from the start of the chapter that summarizes Gen 4 to Exod 18. How does this summary help us understand the concepts of this book (e.g., the CREATOR-creature Distinction, Problem of Sin, and the Organism of Scripture)? How might this enrich our appreciation for the person and work of Christ?

b. What does it say about God (and ultimately the gospel of Christ) that he redeems his people from slavery, reveals himself as Father, and allows his people to experience his presence *before* establishing the Mosaic covenant, laws, and tabernacle?

c. How does this chapter help you understand the Mosaic covenant, laws, and tabernacle as *intended*? In other words, what do these three reveal about God's character and promises, and ultimately Jesus?

d. Go through each of the "commandments" or "words" of the Decalogue (Exod 20:1–17) and apply the law diagram. How does this deepen your appreciation for God's character and promises?

4

Christ as the True David
(Ruth 4, 1 Sam 16–17, 2 Sam 7)

Whether it is the lighthearted *Maleficent* or the more troubling *Joker*, origin stories have captivated people's imagination. Origin stories provide a perspective into why and how certain characters turn out the way that they are. Thus, one of the suspenseful questions in *The Great Gatsby* is the origin of Jay Gatsby. How did he accumulate so much wealth? What is his family background?

David's origin story is central to the way Scripture portrays him. However, we must be once again disciplined in applying the approach:

1. The Creator-creature Distinction reminds us that David's origin story is less about himself and more about God. After all, God, not David, is the main character. In any movie, if we were to associate random side characters as the main character, then it will be impossible to appreciate the plot!

2. The Problem of Sin is not as directly relevant in the passages that we cover. However, the Problem of Sin is always relevant in our own hearts. As we prayerfully engage in God's word through the Spirit, we must recognize that we can easily twist his revelation to be about something other than his character and promises.

3. As we are being trained in seeing God as the main character, we behold not only his glory but the Organism of Scripture. Although every

side character is merely a window into God's character and promises, they nonetheless make unique contributions. David, in many ways, is what Adam and Israel were supposed to be and a foreshadowing of what Christ will be. However, when understanding David as the side character and God as the main character, we see David's deficiencies more clearly, which deepens our appreciation for Christ—specifically his death and resurrection.

In this chapter, we first provide a brief summary from where we last left off to where we are now in the plot of Scripture (Leviticus to 1 Samuel). Then we use the approach to exegete three passages from David's life: his origin account (1 Sam 16:1–13), his battle against Goliath (1 Sam 17), and the covenant that God establishes with him, known as the Davidic covenant (2 Sam 7:1–16). All these passages are narratives, but the first one alludes to David's genealogy. Thus, this chapter also shows how this approach can be applied for all genealogies in Scripture.

SETTING UP DAVID (EXOD 19—1 SAM 15)

In case we are unfamiliar with this portion of Scripture, this section provides a sample of how to apply the approach to passages that have transpired since chapter 3:

Passage	Indicatives	Imperatives	Fulfillment
Exod 19–40	God delivers Israel from Egypt through mighty signs, blesses Israel with a new identity, establishes a covenant with Israel, reveals his character and promises through the law, provides the tabernacle to share his presence with Israel, etc.	Israel to trust in God for all their provision.	The golden calf failure (Exod 32–34) is representative of Israel's heart before the Lord. Yet God still maintains the covenant and blesses Israel with his presence (Exod 40:34–38).
Lev 1–27	God provides sacrificial and purification laws so that Israel's sins can be perpetually forgiven and they may enjoy God's presence (Lev 1–17); also provides the Holiness Code so that Israel can live according to their new identity (Lev 18–27); etc.	Israel to interpret the Levitical law as a window into God's character and promises.	Israel spurns God's law, even the priests (Lev 10, 24:10–16). Later Israel regards God's gift of the sacrificial system as wearisome, offering lame and blind animals (Mal 1).

Passage	Indicatives	Imperatives	Fulfillment
Num 1–25	God fulfills his promise by making Israel very numerous (Num 1); organizing the people (Num 2–5); making provisions for them (Num 7); reminding them of the Passover (Num 9); securing military victories (Num 21); protecting them from Balak (Num 22–24); etc.	Israel to trust and live according to all that God has provided them.	Israel continually grumbles, doubts, rebels, and commits idolatry against God.
Num 26—Deut 34	God raises another generation of Israel who is just as numerous (Num 26); reminds them of his faithfulness (Num 33); outlines how to divide up the promised land (Num 35–36), which implies that he will provide the promised land despite the rebellion of the first generation; delivers a farewell speech through Moses and reminds them of the law so that Israel can prosper (Deut 1–34); etc.	Israel to remember God's trustworthiness as they get ready to possess the promised land.	Not determined until Joshua.
Joshua, Judges, Ruth	God provides the promised land through impossible military victories; raises leaders; continually forgives Israel for their perpetual idolatry; rescues Israel from repeated foreign oppression; sustains the promises/covenants; etc.	Israel to trust God by following his law and depending on him.	Israel only partially obeys, falls into idolatry, persistently forgets the Lord, becomes more corrupt than the Canaanites, etc.
1 Sam 1–15	God is patient with the wickedness of Israel's leaders; raises Samuel to lead; still provides military victories; sets aside David to be a righteous king; etc.	Israel to place their hope in God and not in what they see.	The priesthood becomes corrupt, Israel treats the ark of the covenant with irreverence, the people reject God as their king, they place their hope in other things, etc.

The two patterns that we note in the last chapter are worth revisiting since they have developed in ways that reveal God's character and promises with greater depth. First, God maintains his promises, not because of his people but despite them. This point becomes increasingly clearer throughout the story of Scripture. The people fail more miserably; God's long-suffering love proves to be inexhaustible. When applying this approach throughout these passages, not only do we behold God as the main character, but we notice that these stories are not random. Similarities and patterns become more recognizable.

Second, we saw that there were few instances of trust in the earlier portion of Scripture. But these instances of trust wane significantly as the story of Scripture unfolds. Moreover, positive instances of trust come from individuals whom we least expect, while distrust comes from those whom we would expect to have trusted. Notice the following examples where two side characters are compared, to illustrate this point:

Trust	Unexpected Traits	Distrust	Expected Traits
Rahab	Canaanite prostitute	Achan	Israelite from the tribe of Judah
Ruth	Moabite	Naomi	Israelite from the tribe of Judah
Samuel	Son of a barren woman	Hophni and Phinehas	Priests, sons of Eli the priest
David	Shepherd boy, eighth son	Saul	Handsome, tall; from a wealthy family

Now that we have a brief summary of what has transpired since the last chapter, we can explore what Scripture reveals about God through David.

DAVID'S ORIGIN STORY (1 SAM 16:1-13)

David is introduced in the context of a royal failure. The character flaws of the current king, Saul, are patent. Like Adam, Saul distorts, suppresses, and rejects God's character and promises. And like Adam, the consequences of Saul's disobedience have a cascading effect on those whom he represents. Thus, the prophet Samuel is grieving over Saul's downfall. It is in this dismal situation that God instructs Samuel to find the next king: "I will send you to Jesse the Bethlehemite, for I have provided for myself a king among his sons" (1 Sam 16:1).

There are three details of this instruction that reveal much about God's character and promises:

1. God mentions Jesse. There is nothing noteworthy about Jesse. In many ways, Jesse is like Abram or Moses—a random person whom

God chooses. The insignificance of these side character further cement God's willingness to interact with people who do not deserve his attention.

Although Jesse is insignificant, this is not the first time that his name appears in Scripture. This same Jesse is mentioned twice in the conclusion of the book of Ruth:

> And the women of the neighborhood gave him a name, saying, "A son has been born to Naomi." They named him Obed. He was the father of *Jesse*, the father of David. (Ruth 4:17)

> Obed fathered *Jesse*, and *Jesse* fathered David. (Ruth 4:22)

Ruth is a beautifully written book on many levels, but it ends with a genealogy. If we do not understand genealogies in the Bible as God intends, then we might think that ending such a compelling story with a genealogy is a mistake. This, then, raises the question of the importance and purpose of genealogies, which we cover in the next section.

Before reading further about the second detail, take a moment to read 1 Sam 16:1–4a according to the covenantal/iterative flow (the indicative-imperative-fulfillment triad). Are you able to see all three aspects in these verses?

2. God gives the reason for his commandment through the conjunction "for." This word is from the Hebrew *ki*, which signifies the purpose or reason. The reason for Samuel to go to Jesse (imperative) is that God has already provided for himself a king (indicative). Thus, in this verse, we see an indicative-imperative-fulfillment triad:

   a. Indicatives:
      1. God notices that Samuel has been grieving: "How long will you grieve over Saul?" (1 Sam 16:1a).
      2. God already has a plan: "I have provided for myself a king" (1 Sam 16:1c; see also 1 Sam 16:2–3).

   b. Imperative:
      1. How Samuel can benefit from the indicatives: by going "to Jesse the Bethlehemite" (1 Sam 16:1b).

The triad helps us notice that God empathizes with Samuel and already has a plan for the next king. Therefore, the imperative to go to

Jesse is not so much an onerous command but an invitation to live according to these indicatives. No longer does Samuel have to feel stuck in discouragement; God knows what he's going through and has a plan in which Samuel can participate.

3. God does not specify who the king is. He leaves it generically as one of Jesse's sons ("among his sons," 1 Sam 16:1d).[1] As we see shortly in the genealogy section, there is a pattern in Scripture: God chooses the least likely individuals, not those who are expected to be chosen (e.g., the oldest).[2] This is not because God is an ageist. As this account progresses, God explains why this pattern exists.

Samuel fulfills this indicative-imperative-fulfillment triad by trusting God's indicatives and therefore obeying his imperatives (1 Sam 16:4a). When Samuel arrives at Jesse's house, he sees his oldest son, Eliab. Based on Eliab's appearance, Samuel is convinced that he is the one God has chosen. Here God reveals why he frequently chooses the younger: "Do not look on his appearance or on the height of his stature, because I have rejected him. For the LORD sees not as man sees: man looks on the outward appearance, but the LORD looks on the heart" (1 Sam 16:7).

Essentially, God's standards transcend our human, worldly, fleshly standards. What society esteems might be contrary to what God values. When God says that he "looks on the heart," it is not a generic quality (e.g., positive thinking, persistent hope, etc.). The posture that God has in mind is one that is likelier to live according to the CREATOR-creature Distinction (i.e., to trust and submit to God in humility and dependence). Often, worldly or fleshly attributes (e.g., wealth, status, title, etc.) make it less likely to submit to the CREATOR-creature Distinction.

Since Eliab is not the chosen one, Jesse presents each of his other sons before Samuel, only for all seven of them to be rejected (1 Sam 16:8–10).[3] It is not until Samuel asks, "Are all your sons here?" that Jesse even mentions

---

1. Not specifying concrete details is a pattern in how God relates with his people (e.g., Abram is never told the specific area during his initial calling). This is not because God does not know or because he is being difficult—instead, he is teaching them how to trust him in every step and for their daily bread so that they do not lean on their own understanding.

2. E.g., Abel or Seth over Cain; Shem over Japheth; Isaac over Ishmael; Jacob over Esau; Levi and Judah over Reuben and Simeon; Perez over Zerah; etc.

3. On the discrepancy with 1 Chr 2:13–15, see Long, *1 and 2 Samuel*, 172.

his other son, David (1 Sam 16:11)![4] Even then, Jesse does not even consider David as a possibility: "There remains yet the youngest, but behold, he is keeping the sheep." Samuel has to insist by instructing Jesse: "Send and get him, for we will not sit down till he comes here." Later in this passage David is anointed as king (1 Sam 16:12–13).

There is much more that can be said about this account, but the simple point is that David's origin story is not about himself. There is nothing significant about David, as his very own father attests! What his origin story does reveal, however, is God's character and promises. This is yet another one of the countless examples where God chooses the forgotten. This is because God empathizes with the humble and the weak. But this is also to stress that the independent God alone is the main character. Thus, everyone else is merely a side character whose function is to reflect the glory of the main character. The practical implications of this can be quite frustrating for those who are immature and resist the CREATOR-creature Distinction. But as we mature and come to grips with reality, we recognize that this is a glorious dynamic. For who else deserves such attention and affection? So as much as this is a biblical pattern, we must ask ourselves if this is the way we live Scripture and read life.

GENEALOGIES

One of the more common frustrations with our engagement with God's word is misunderstanding genealogies. This frustration is significant because there are quite a few genealogies, and they serve a very important role. We fall into one of two extremes regarding genealogies: either disregard them as fillers or overinterpret them by being fixated on tangential details.

This, then, raises the questions of why there are so many genealogies in the Bible and how to understand them as intended. Some have suggested that the purpose of genealogies is to convey the historicity of the Bible, to confirm the fulfillment of prophecies, and/or to provide details about interesting characters (e.g., Enoch [Gen 5:24]; Jabez [1 Chr 4:9–10]). As much as these are valid, they miss the essence of genealogies since all of God's revelation is primarily about himself.

In the subsections below, we learn about (a) the nature of other genealogies, (b) how biblical genealogies differ, and (c) some of the purposes

---

4. Cue the "Am I a joke to you?" meme.

of biblical genealogies in order to (d) understand genealogies as a window into God's character and promises. Once we establish these basic principles, we apply them to the genealogy of Jesse/David in Ruth 4 so that we can understand it as intended.

Genealogies in General

Scholars have researched genealogies of the ancient Near East as well as modern verbal genealogies. Without getting too technical, here is a brief summary:[5]

1. The purpose of most genealogies, especially in the ancient Near East, is to express domestic (e.g., social order, position, status), political (e.g., list of kings), or religious (e.g., priests) relationships.

2. Genealogies are often used as a literary tool and can be understood as their own genre. They are often used to move a narrative forward.

3. The purpose of genealogies is therefore not primarily for historical accuracy, though they do provide much historical value.

4. Most genealogies are patrilinear (i.e., they trace the male figures; females are typically not mentioned).

Distinctiveness of Biblical Genealogies

When we understand the characteristics of genealogies in the ancient Near East and other cultures, we can appreciate the distinctiveness of biblical genealogies:

1. While ancient Near Eastern genealogies usually list only one descendent (known as "linear"), biblical genealogies usually list more than one descendent (known as "segmented").

2. Ancient Near Eastern genealogies seek to legitimize an individual; biblical genealogies often show the shortcomings of individuals (when there are positive examples, like Enoch [Gen 5:24] and Jabez [1 Chr

---

5. For more details, see Wilson, *Genealogy and History*; Hess, "Genealogies of Genesis 1–11"; John H. Walton, "Genealogies," in Arnold and Williamson, *Historical Books*, 309–16; Dawson et al., *All the Genealogies*.

4:9–10], the focus is not on the individual but their relationship with God).

3. If there is a central theme that captures the purpose of all the genealogies of Scripture, it is that God is faithful to his promises—that is, they emphasize the trustworthiness of God's character. Thus, even in genealogies, we see that God alone is the main character.

Royal and Priestly Genealogies

Most of the biblical genealogies are in the Old Testament. One of the reasons for this is the importance of tracing the kingly and priestly lines. So in the largest genealogy section of the Bible (1 Chr 1–9), the tribes that are responsible for kings and priests contain the most information. The kings come from the tribe of Judah, which makes up one hundred of the verses (1 Chr 2:3—4:23); the priests come from the tribe of Levi, which makes up eighty-one verses (1 Chr 6). The other tribes make up one to twenty verses each. It was crucial to maintain the accuracy of these lineages so that Israel could determine who was a legitimate king and priest.

Genealogies as a Window to God's Character and Promises

One of the reasons why biblical genealogies can feel challenging is that they typically list more names (since some are "segmented" [e.g., Gen 10, Num 26:5–51] and not just "linear" [e.g., Gen 5]). For modern readers, this might be an annoyance, but we must be trained to consider what these additional names imply about God's character and promises.

As we saw in how God commands Samuel to go to the house of Jesse, God does not operate based on worldly standards. God could have easily chosen the oldest child, Eliab. Instead, God tells Samuel that it is someone "among his sons" (1 Sam 16:1). Similarly, one of the unusual aspects of biblical genealogies is that they contain more than one descendent ("segmented"). That God includes more names indicates at least the following about his character and promises:

1. God cares about more than just the people who are prominent. We see this more emphatically in how the Torah makes many provisions for those who are marginalized (e.g., the widows, orphans, and sojourners) and how Jesus intentionally seeks the outcasts of society.

2. God's care for all people is in part because he is love. It is also in part because every human is created in his image, which is rare in other worldviews or religions, especially in the ancient Near East.[6] This is especially the case as God includes the genealogy of the line of Cain, a lineage that is overall rebellious toward God (Gen 4:17–24).

3. God is maintaining the gift of life and procreation.[7] This goes all the way back to God's original command that is referred to as the cultural mandate: "Be fruitful and multiply and fill the earth" (Gen 1:28–30). Thus, it makes sense for him to "keep the receipts" of all those whom he has been blessed with the gift of life. Indeed, it is quite shocking that God preserves the ability for humans to procreate and experience life even after Adam and Eve's sin, which should have resulted in death (Gen 2:16–17).

4. Similarly, God is faithful to fulfill his promises no matter how tenuous they seem. For instance, God promises a seed of Eve to be the vindicator (Gen 3:15). Every genealogy is a reminder that God will fulfill this promise even in the face of humanity's fragility and sin. Cain's genealogy represents a line that rebels against God (Gen 4:17–24). Parallel to Cain's genealogy is that of Seth, which shows that there are ten generations between Adam and Noah (Gen 5). By the time of Noah, "every intention of the thoughts of [humanity's] heart was only evil continually" (Gen 6:5). What does all this say about God? God patiently gives humanity the gift of life and procreation through all those generations despite humanity's commitment to sin. Even after the flood, humanity is still committed to evil (Gen 8:21). Yet there is still another genealogy after the flood in Gen 10 (known as the Table of Nations) that implies that God is still mercifully sustaining humanity so that he can fulfill his promise to Adam (Gen 3:15).

One of the metaphors for all the biblical genealogies is that of a tree of life (e.g., Exod 15:13–17, Isa 60:21, Ps 92:12–14).[8] So even though Adam and Eve are not permitted to eat from *the* tree of life in the garden of Eden,

---

6. In the ancient Near East, the image of God would be applicable only to kings except in the Egyptian *Instruction of Merikare* (Walton, *Ancient Near Eastern Thought*, 212).

7. Surely this is a provision that we take for granted, thus making stories like *The Handmaid's Tale* and *The Children of Men* compelling.

8. Dawson et al., *All the Genealogies*, xxiv.

God has nonetheless given them the gift of life and procreation so that they are the originator of many trees of life!

The Specific Genealogy of Ruth 4

Now that we have established some of the context for understanding biblical genealogies as intended, we can now apply it to Ruth 4. As mentioned above, the reference to "Jesse the Bethlehemite" is significant (1 Sam 16:1). But the significance does not lie in Jesse or Bethlehem—it lies in God.

Ruth concludes with a genealogy where Jesse is mentioned. Thus 1 Samuel is making a reference to another book of the Bible (this is known as *intertextuality*, where there is a link to another text—thus, "inter-" and "-textuality"). As a visual summary, this is the genealogy in Ruth 4:17–22, with reference to what we observed in 1 Sam 16:[9]

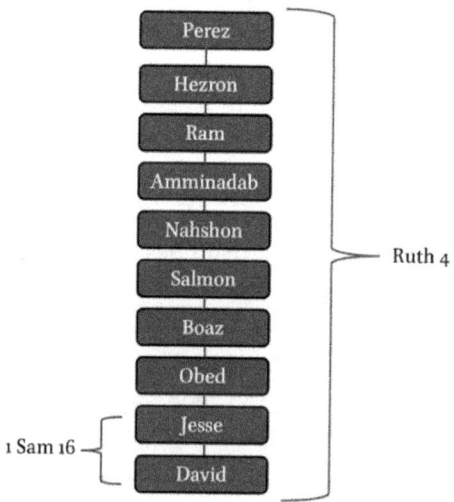

Due to limitations of space, we look only at three individuals and their background: Perez, Salmon, and Boaz. For genealogies, intertextuality is going to be crucial. The more we are familiar with other parts of Scripture, the more we can appreciate the significance of these individuals and their background.

---

9. The genealogy begins and ends with the Obed-Jesse-David relationship (Ruth 4:17 and 22), so this would be another inclusio. This implies that the focus of this genealogy is on the Obed-Jesse-David portion.

Perez

The oldest individual mentioned in this genealogy is Perez. Perez's origin story is from Gen 38. Perez is the twin brother of Zerah, both being born of Tamar and Judah. The relationship between Tamar and Judah is scandalous because Tamar is actually Judah's daughter-in-law!

Judah, from whom all Israel's kings come, is one of the twelve sons of Israel/Jacob. Judah has three sons: Er, Onan, and Shelah. Er is the husband of Tamar, but Er dies without children because he is wicked before the LORD. According to the custom of the time, Onan is supposed to bear a child with Tamar in order to extend the line of Er. So Onan has sex with Tamar but does not ejaculate into her. The LORD regards this as reprehensible, so he puts Onan to death. This leaves only Shelah as Judah's offspring.

Instead of offering Shelah to Tamar, Judah tricks Tamar. So Tamar pretends to be a prostitute, and Judah has sex with her and produces twins, Zerah and Perez. The line through which Israel's kings are produced, which includes David and eventually Jesus, is from Perez. This is indeed a shocking detail. Perez is not even the older of the two twins, and he is born of the shameful relationship of a father and his daughter-in-law. In this origin story, there is nothing noble about Perez or his parents. Below is how Gen 38 adds to the genealogy of Ruth 4:

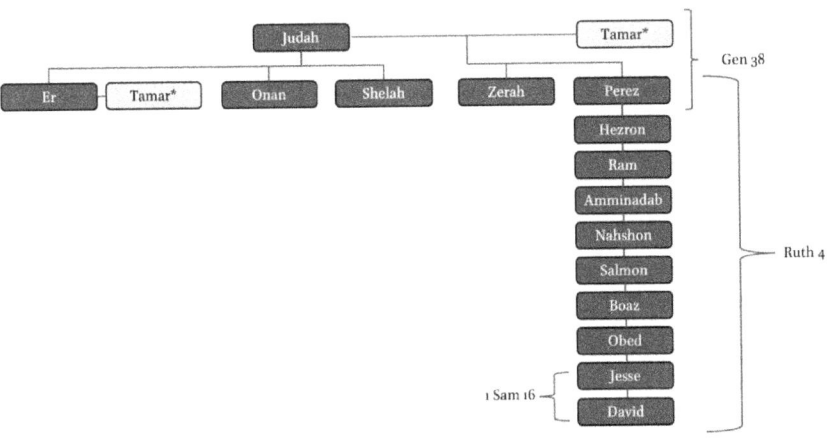

Salmon

Salmon's origin story is not neatly captured in one chapter. Instead, it is pieced together through Josh 2:1–21, 6:17–25; Ruth 4:20–21; and Matt 1:5. The key to understanding Salmon is understanding his wife, Rahab.

Rahab is introduced as a Canaanite prostitute (Josh 2:1–21). She, like all the other Canaanites, is supposed to be destroyed by Israel because rather than repenting, the Canaanites persist in their wickedness toward God for centuries (Gen 15:16). Rahab, however, hears of God's character and promises, and out of trust, she decides to help Israel. Israel, in return, ensures that Rahab and her household do not suffer the same fate as the rest of the Canaanites (Josh 6:17–25). Thus, Rahab turns from being a Canaanite prostitute to being part of God's people; in fact, she becomes part of Israel's royalty! On the other hand, Rahab is juxtaposed with Achan—he is not only born an Israelite but is part of the prestigious line of Judah, yet he blatantly disregards God's explicit command (Josh 7). Once again, there is nothing virtuous about Salmon. The only redeeming quality is from his wife, who is a Canaanite prostitute. What is highlighted from Rahab is that she submits to God's character and promises. Thus, like the origin story of Perez, Salmon's background also highlights God. Here is a visual summary of how Rahab is grafted into Perez's line:

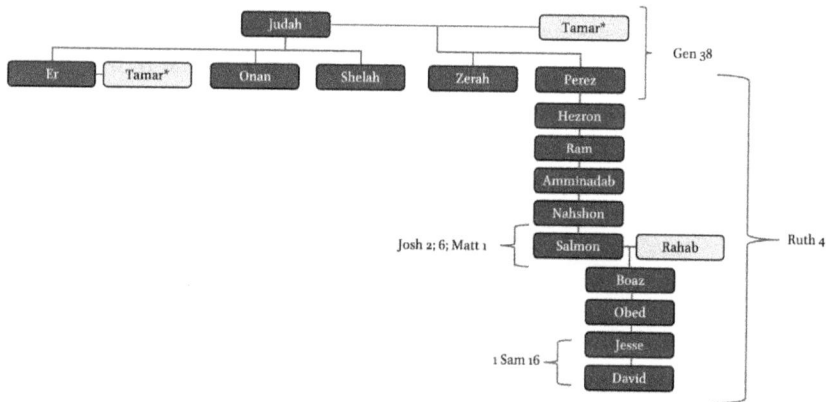

Boaz

As is the case for Perez and Salmon, the key to understanding Boaz is to understand the woman in his life—his wife, Ruth—which is captured in the book of Ruth.

Ruth is a Moabite, so she, like Rahab, should have been destroyed along with the Canaanites. However, Ruth marries an Israelite named Mahlon, so she becomes part of the people of God. The book of Ruth begins with a famine in Judah, so her household migrates to Moab (Ruth

1:1–5). Sadly Mahlon, his brother, and his father all die without producing children. This, then, leaves only Ruth, her mother-in-law (Naomi), and her sister-in-law (Orpah, who is another Moabite). When Naomi hears that the famine has ended, she and Ruth go back to Judah while Orpah stays in Moab (Ruth 1:6).

Naomi, who is an Israelite, is bitter at God, so she changes her name to Mara (Ruth 1:20). Ruth, however, places her trust in God. Eventually Ruth meets Boaz, who is eligible to marry her (Ruth 2:19–20). Only at the end of Ruth do we find out that Boaz is a descendent of Perez—Tamar's son (Ruth 4:18–22). More specifically, Boaz is the son of Salmon. So Ruth becomes the daughter-in-law of Rahab and Salmon—enabling Ruth to be part of future royalty! Ruth and Boaz produce Obed, who is the grandfather of David.

Once again, the origin story of Boaz accentuates who God is. Only God can use famines, premature deaths, bitterness, widowhood, and other unfavorable circumstances as parts of an eternal plan of salvation that will produce not only David but the True David—Jesus Christ. We can now have a fuller appreciation for God's faithfulness based on this genealogy:

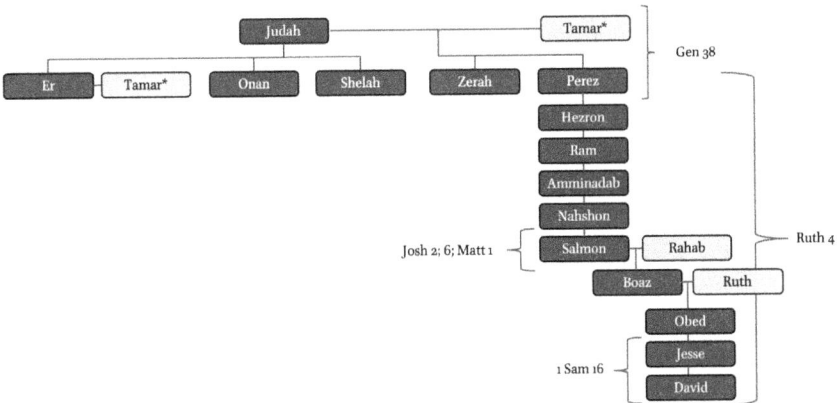

Summary

Each of the stories is quite fascinating. There are many compelling aspects of these individuals. However, the purpose of this book is to help us remember that God is the main character and that all of reality, including these origin stories, are windows into his character and promises. So we must take a step back and reflect upon what can we learn about God through these accounts:

1. Each of the narratives above can be understood through the narrative diagram. There we see that God is trustworthy and faithful despite the deceit of Judah, Er, and Onan; the willful disobedience of Achan; or the bitterness of Naomi. All God is asking of his people is to trust in him.

2. Each of these narratives contains elements of shame—whether it's the incestuous sexual relations, the vocation of prostitution, or being a people of idolatry. Yet there is no embarrassment that God cannot handle. God includes these obscene details about the very people whom he chooses in order to emphasize that we are never too far from the reach of his kindness.

3. As mentioned earlier, there is a tension between worldly standards and God's standards. From a fleshly standpoint, there is nothing virtuous about Tamar, Perez, Rahab, or Ruth. In fact, each of them should be written off and is compared with individuals who are expected to be positive examples: Judah, Achan, and Naomi. God seeks those who live according to the CREATOR-creature Distinction. Often, this attitude comes from those who are least expected, while those who appear to have it all together are most resistant.

4. Relatedly, the central side character of each of the accounts above is a woman.[10] This is quite rare not only in ancient Near Eastern narratives but also in genealogies, since most genealogies are patrilinear. We see in the next chapter that the most important genealogy of Scripture unexpectedly mentions the names of women, including Tamar, Rahab, and Ruth (Matt 1:3–5)!

5. God is faithful despite the fragility of humanity. From a human standpoint, Judah's line is on the brink of demise multiple times (e.g., Gen 38). Somehow, God grafts unexpected people—Rahab, the Canaanite prostitute, and Ruth, the Moabite—to not only Israel, but to the line of Judah. If God's covenants were up to humanity, then they would be broken immediately (e.g., Exod 32–34). Nevertheless these covenants are fulfilled only because God's trustworthiness endures. Though

---

10. For a comprehensive study on women in the ancient Near East, see Stol, *Women in the Ancient Near East*.

God's promises feel like they hang on a thread, Scripture reassures us that there is a certainty because he is the faithful promise keeper. God accomplishes his purposes not because of us but despite us. Hence, all glory belongs to him alone!

6. We see more clearly in the next chapter that all genealogies are ultimately fulfilled in Christ. The two prominent lines of the Old Testament—priestly and kingly—are fulfilled by Christ because he is the everlasting high priest and the True David. Thus, after the fulfillment of Christ, genealogies are no longer maintained in Scripture (e.g., 1 Tim 1:4, Titus 3:9). The death and resurrection of Christ are foundational in this regard. All the shame and guilt that these genealogies record are tolerated by God because they are eventually paid by the death of Christ; all the positive examples of trust and obedience in these genealogies foreshadow the perfect righteousness of Christ that is shared with his people through his resurrection. This table provides some examples:

Side Character	Jesus Christ
Enoch walks with God (Gen 5:24).	Christ has an eternal/perfect relationship with the Father and Spirit (e.g., Matt 3:17, 17:5).
Noah provides temporary relief from the toil of labor (Gen 5:29).	Christ secures eternal rest from sin (Heb 3:7—4:13).
Jabez prays for blessings upon himself (1 Chr 4:9–10).	Christ prays for blessings upon his people (Rom 8:34).

If God is pleased with Enoch, Noah, Jabez, and others, how much more is he pleased with Christ? And since the righteousness of Christ has been shared with us, how much should we celebrate Christ?

How to Understand Other Genealogies

The purpose of this book is not merely to offer exegesis on certain passages but an approach that can be applied to other passages. Here are some of the key steps that can be applied to other genealogies:

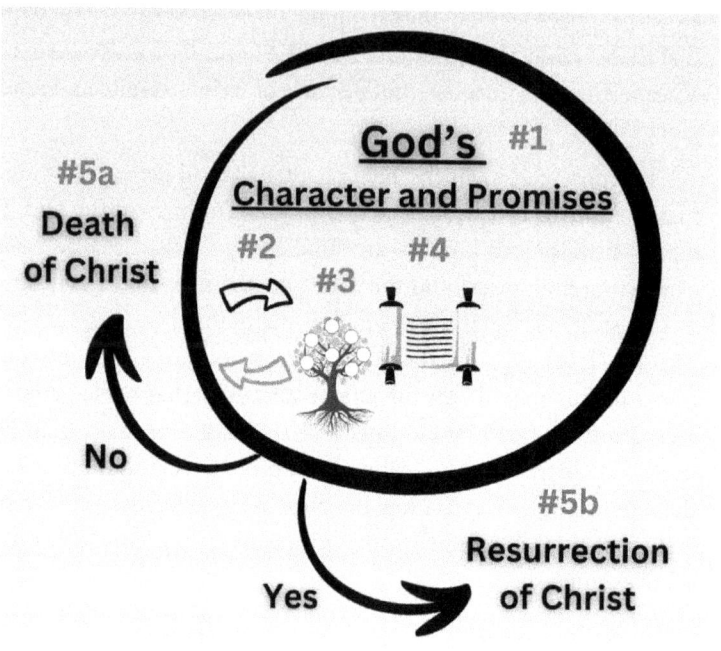

#1	Remember that genealogies, like all of Scripture and reality, are a window to God's character and promises.
#2	What comes before and after the genealogy? Does the placement of the genealogy imply anything about God's character and promises?
#3	Are there details about any of the individuals? As much as these might be intriguing, take a step back and reflect on what these details say about God.
#4	Familiarize yourself with the names. Have you seen these names before? See if there are any cross references to these names. If so, then look up their backstory (intertextuality). Their backstory is usually a narrative, so you can apply the narrative diagram.
#5	If there are negative examples from #3 or #4, then they are addressed for God's people through the death of Christ (#5a); if positive, then they foreshadow the perfect righteousness that Christ fulfills and that is shared with his people through his resurrection (#5b).

Similar to the narrative diagram, the purpose of genealogies is to highlight God's trustworthiness. He is faithful to fulfill and keep his promises and covenants—not because of the side characters but despite them.

Now that we are equipped to see biblical genealogies as intended and understand the purpose of David's origin story, we explore two events of David's life: the battle with Goliath and the Davidic covenant.

DAVID AND GOLIATH (1 SAM 17)

"David and Goliath" might be the most popular reference to Scripture, but it is also one that is often misunderstood. It is a common way to describe any situation where the odds are stacked against you. Like all things, we warp God's revelation, which is intended to highlight himself, into something else—whether a feel-good story, inspiration for underdogs, or an example of creatively transforming disadvantages into advantages. One of the values of this book is to exemplify how to read Scripture as intended. Hence, as we engage in God's word with him being the main character and the backgrounds of Adam and Israel fresh on our minds, we can enjoy the fruit of understanding this famous account correctly.

Before reading further below, read 1 Sam 17 yourself and apply the narrative diagram:

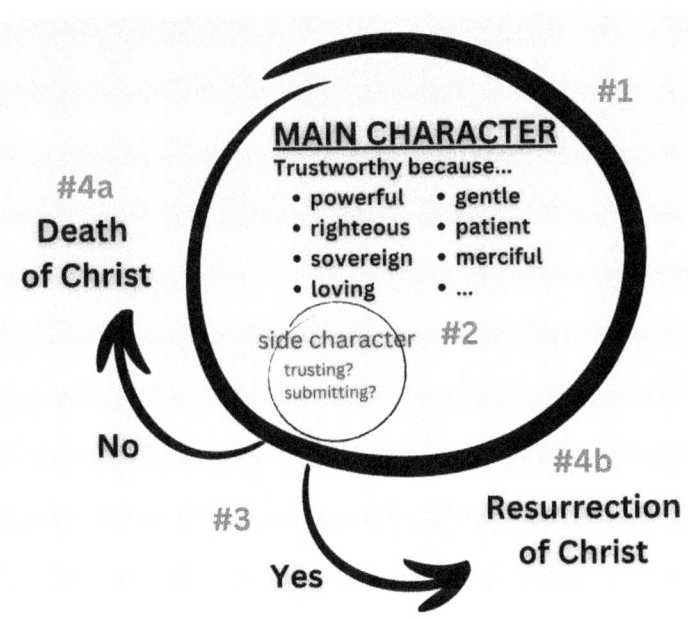

Here is a sample of how the narrative diagram can be applied for 1 Sam 17:

#		
#1	**The Trustworthiness of the Main Character:** God has proven his faithfulness through several generations since Abraham: fulfilling the Abrahamic promises, delivering Israel from Egypt, providing food and water miraculously, appearing to Israel through a pillar of cloud and fire, defeating all of Israel's enemies, providing Israel with the promised land, etc. More personally, God has been faithful to David as he has protected his sheep in the face of lions and bears (1 Sam 17:34–37).	Indicative
#2	**God's Invitation:** In the light of all the indicatives (#1) and the fact that Israel is cowering in fear, David has the opportunity to fight Goliath (1 Sam 17:31–37).	Imperative
#3	**The Side Character's Trust:** David's exclusive trust in God is shown in what he says (1 Sam 17:34–37, 45–47) and by forsaking the sword and armor (17:39). God delivers victory through this act of trust (17:49–54).	Fulfillment
#4	**Christ's Fulfillment:** #4b is highlighted in this example. As inspirational as David's trust is, he is merely the side character, and his trust foreshadows Christ's perfect obedience. While David's trust secures temporary military victory over the Philistines, Christ secures everlasting holistic victory over sin and death. While David slays the one who defies God's name, Christ himself is slain to save those who defy God's name (so #4a is still relevant). Christ's perfect trust and obedience are necessary for the efficacy of his death, have been imputed to his people through his resurrection, and are that to which his people are being conformed. In sum, we see that David's obedience cannot satisfy God's requirements since it only yields temporary victory; Christ's obedience fully satisfies God's requirements.	Fulfillment

Creator-Creature Distinction

Like every part of reality, the best way of understanding the intended significance of the battle between David and Goliath is in the context of the Creator-creature Distinction. This immediately exposes the superficiality of all other interpretations of this passage. The passage itself provides clues that the battle is not so much between David and Goliath or even the Israelites and the Philistines. Rather, the heart of the battle is the name and glory of God. Everyone other than David is interpreting the situation through fleshly factors (e.g., the military aspect). Only David recognizes the true conflict because only he is approaching the situation according to the CREATOR-creature Distinction. This becomes apparent when we study what David says. Notice how his concern is that God is being defied and how his motivation and confidence orbit around God:

> What shall be done for the man who kills this Philistine and takes away the reproach from Israel? For who is *this uncircumcised Philistine*, that **he should defy the armies of the living God**? (1 Sam 17:26)

> Your servant used to keep sheep for his father. And when there came a lion, or a bear, and took a lamb from the flock, I went after him and struck him and delivered it out of his mouth. And if he arose against me, I caught him by his beard and struck him and killed him. Your servant has struck down both lions and bears, and *this uncircumcised Philistine* shall be like one of them, **for he has defied the armies of the living God.** . . . The LORD who delivered me from the paw of the lion and from the paw of the bear will deliver me from the hand of this Philistine. (1 Sam 17:34–37)

> You come to me with a sword and with a spear and with a javelin, but **I come to you in the name of the LORD of hosts, the God of the armies of Israel, whom you have defied.** This day the LORD will deliver you into my hand, and I will strike you down and cut off your head. And I will give the dead bodies of the host of the Philistines this day to the birds of the air and to the wild beasts of the earth, that all the earth may know that there is a God in Israel, and that all this assembly may know that the LORD saves not with sword and spear. For the battle is the LORD's, and he will give you into our hand. (1 Sam 17:45–47)

David is essentially saying that God is the main character. If his name is being defied, then something needs to be done—regardless of what the odds are. In fact, since God has proven himself to be powerful, trustworthy, and loving, the odds are against Goliath and the Philistines!

1. In the *italicized* text, David does not even utter the name "Goliath." Instead, he refers to him as "this uncircumcised Philistine" (1 Sam 17:26, 36). Uncircumcision is important because that implies the person is outside of God's people (circumcision was the sign of the Abrahamic covenant in Gen 17). Thus, David's frame of reference when assessing Goliath is not his physical stature or his warrior attributes.

Instead, his frame of reference is God. Since Goliath is uncircumcised, he does not have the promises of God on his side.[11]

2. In the **bold** text, David fixates on the fact that Goliath has defied God. The verb "defy" comes from the Hebrew *charaf*, which occurs a total of five times in this account (17:10, 25, 26, 36, 45; also the noun form in 17:26). Hence, God's honor is the central motivation for David. David's willingness to fight is not about his bravery or the need to be a hero; it is simply a response to God's name being defied.

3. In the underlined text, David is placing his confidence in God. His confidence is not in himself or a vague sense of optimism. Instead, he knows who God is. He trusts and submits to the fact that God has been faithful to him in the past, so he will therefore be faithful to him in this current situation. However, it is not a confidence that is based on David or even Israel, but on the fact that God will not allow his name to be defied (**bold text**) by someone who is not even part of the covenant (*italicized text*).

Yet again, when we see God as the rightful main character of every passage, certain patterns become noticeable. In the following subsections, we see David portrayed in similar ways as the previous side characters of Adam and Israel—thus, we see more of the Organism of Scripture.

In the Light of Adam

As we saw in chapter 1, Adam is given authority over all of God's creation (Gen 1:26, 28–30; 2:19–20). So like David, Adam is portrayed as a kingly figure. More specifically, Adam has dominion over all the creatures. Yet the tragic twist is that Adam succumbs to the serpent. David also shows his dominion over creatures. Unlike Adam, David uses his authority over the animals as God intends. As a faithful shepherd, David protects the sheep by subduing predators like lions and bears (1 Sam 17:34–37).

More importantly, both Adam and David are confronted with a situation where someone is defying God. In Adam's situation, the serpent misleads Eve into distorting, suppressing, and ultimately rejecting God's character and promises. Adam cowardly watches and eventually complies. In David's situation, it is precisely the defiance of God that ignites him to

---

11. This is the same language that Jonathan uses in the miraculous victory that he experiences (1 Sam 14:6).

take action. From a human standpoint, Adam had every advantage while David had every disadvantage.

The serpent and Goliath share other similarities beyond defying God's name. Goliath is depicted as a snakelike figure.[12] The details regarding Goliath stress that he is covered in bronze, which, in the Hebrew, shares the same root as the Hebrew word for serpent (*nechshet* and *nachash*). The word is used five times (1 Sam 17:5 [x2], 17:6 [x2], 17:38). Not only is his helmet made of bronze but so is his leg armor and his javelin (1 Sam 17:5–6). In other words, he is covered head to toe in bronze. Each time the Hebrew word for bronze is heard, it sounds like the word for serpent. Additionally, Goliath is "armed with a coat of mail" (17:5). The Hebrew word for "mail" is *qasqeset*, whose primary meaning is "scale," like that of fish (Lev 11:9, Deut 14:9) or serpents (Ezek 29:3–4). So as people hear the details of this narrative, they visualize Goliath as a serpent.[13]

Furthermore, Scripture provides details about how Goliath dies that allude to the curse on the serpent:

> He [Goliath] fell on his face to the ground. (1 Sam 17:49b)

> . . . and dust you shall eat
> all the days of your life. (Gen 3:14b)

The image for both is that each of their wickedness results in having their face on the ground. Accordingly, the word "head," in reference to Goliath being decapitated, is emphasized (1 Sam 17:46, 51, 54, 57). This emphasis brings to attention the serpent's "head" that is to be bruised: "He shall bruise your head" (Gen 3:15a).

In summary, Adam and David are both confronted with an adversary. In each, the adversary is depicted similarly (i.e., defying God's character and promises, and scaly/serpentlike). The essential difference between Adam and David is living according to the CREATOR-creature Distinction—cowardice and bravery are merely by-products.

---

12. See also Verrett, *Serpent in Samuel*.

13. Another example from Scripture would be 2 Kgs 18:4, where most footnotes indicate that the Hebrew for *bronze* and *serpent* sound alike.

In the Light of Israel

Like Adam, God has blessed Israel with a privileged identity (firstborn son, treasured possession), which includes kingly attributes (royal priesthood and holy nation). If Adam trusted and submitted to God, his dominion would have extended, benefiting the rest of creation. Similarly, if Israel trusted and submitted to God, they would fulfill their identity, being a blessing to all the nations as God had promised to Abraham (Gen 12:1–3). God has proven his faithfulness to Israel through the ten signs and the parting of the Red Sea.

In the same way, God has given David a privileged identity (anointing him as king in 1 Sam 16:1–13) and has proven his faithfulness to him by delivering him from bears and lions (1 Sam 17:34–37). Another connection between Israel and David is the emphasis on circumcision. David regards Goliath as "this uncircumcised Philistine" (1 Sam 17:26, 36)—someone outside of God's people. Circumcision is the sign of the Abrahamic covenant (Gen 17:10–14) and becomes the most prominent mark of Israel.[14] Therefore, circumcision is mentioned at key junctures of Israel's history: before the ten signs of Egypt (Exod 4:24–26) and before the military victories into the promised land (Josh 5:1–9). So circumcision is a reminder to Israel of the gracious covenant that God has made with them—that he is their God and that they are his people.

But as mentioned in chapter 3, Israel fails just like Adam as soon as Israel has an opportunity. In Exod 32, Israel does not trust and submit to God's character and promises; instead, they trust in what they can see. Both Adam and Israel rely on fleshly factors—namely, sight (Gen 3:6, Exod 32:4–5). This is consistent with how Israel responds to other difficulties. Earlier when Pharaoh makes their slavery more difficult, Israel turns against Moses (Exod 5:21); they accuse Moses of murderous intentions when they face the Red Sea (Exod 14:11–12); and when they are hungry and thirsty, this accusation is directed to God (Exod 16:3, 8; 17:2–7). In all these cases, Israel places more weight on their fleshly senses rather than on God's character and promises. They are operating based on sight and not faith. David, on the other hand, does not view the threat of Goliath with a worldly perspective. Rather, he is interpreting his reality rightfully according to the

---

14. It is important to know that Israel as the people of God is not based on "ethnic" factors as passages like Exod 12:48 make clear. This is explained more fully later in the New Testament (e.g., Gal 4).

CREATOR-creature Distinction. He is placing greater weight in who God is rather than the situation.

Within the Narrative Diagram

All the observations above are more easily recognizable when we apply the approach of this book. Thus, one of the values of this book is that it proffers models and frameworks that can be applied to other passages. Below is the same narrative diagram as well as a table that summarizes the main points.

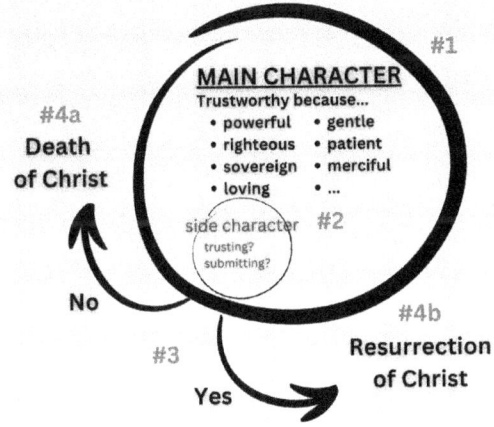

	God and Adam	**God and Israel**	**God and David**
#1. **The Trustworthiness of the Main Character (Indicative)**	God creates Adam in the image of God; blesses Adam with dominion over all his creation; provides Adam with the suitable helper (Eve); and lavishes upon Adam the perfect environment for him to flourish.	God sets aside Israel as his firstborn son; delivers Israel from Egypt through ten signs and the parting of the Red Sea; provides food and water miraculously; gives Israel a new identity; blesses Israel with the Mosaic covenant, the law, and tabernacle.	Even before his birth, God ensures that David's lineage would specifically bring him into existence (e.g., working through Tamar, Rahab, and Ruth); out of all the sons of Jesse, God chooses and anoints David; God shows his faithfulness in David's shepherding.
#2. **God's Invitation (Imperative)**	Adam sees the serpent (over whom he has authority and whom he named) mislead Eve (with whom he is married and is the object of his romance). Moreover, the serpent maligns God's character and promises.	Israel is to place their trust in God's character and promises.	David hears the Philistines defy God's name while all of Israel is cowering in fear.
#3. **The Side Character's Trust (Fulfillment)**	Rather than trusting in God, Adam distorts, suppresses, and rejects God's character and promises. Rather than defending his wife, he leaves her vulnerable and blames her. Rather than exercising his authority over the serpent, he succumbs to its lies about God's character and promises.	Israel places their trust in other things. The chief example is the golden calf incident (Exod 32), but this failure to trust in God is seen throughout Israel's history.	David agrees to fight Goliath to honor God's name and because he is certain of God's faithfulness.

#4. Christ's Fulfillment (Fulfillment)	Adam and Eve (and humanity) are shielded from the full consequences of their sin (#4a). These consequences are eventually addressed by the death of Christ. Instead, God offers promises of redemption—all of the requirements of these promises are secured by the resurrection of Christ (#4b).	Despite Israel's continual rejection of God, God's mercy nonetheless abounds (#4a). He establishes more covenants, provides repeatedly, and is faithful across the generations. Israel's continual rejection is addressed ultimately by the death of Christ. The true solution, which is a new heart, is also provided by Christ through his resurrection (#4b).	David's trust and submission to God are inspirational and foreshadow Christ's perfect righteousness, which is exemplified in his death and confirmed by his resurrection (#4b). David's bravery benefits Israel, conquers Goliath, and secures temporary victory. But Christ's obedience fully satisfies the requirements of God: Christ's bravery benefits all his people, conquers sin and death, and secures everlasting victory through his death and resurrection.

THE DAVIDIC COVENANT (2 SAM 7)

The last part of David that we study in this chapter is the Davidic covenant. We cannot cover every aspect of the Davidic covenant, so below we highlight only the portions that help us understand and apply the concepts from this book. As we see below, the CREATOR-creature Distinction reminds us that everything God does, including establishing covenants, is out of his sovereignty and grace. One of the comforts of the Davidic covenant is that it addresses the Problem of Sin—the inconsistency and fragility of God's people. Lastly, the Organism of Scripture enables us to see how later parts of Scripture develop, crystallize, and extend earlier parts. The reason for this is that God is the main character, so there is unity in his word. As we track this development, the New Testament shows that all of Scripture is grounded, saturated, and culminating in Christ alone.

As It Is Written and Intended

Creator-Creature Distinction

How the covenant is initiated seems odd, but it makes sense through the Creator-creature Distinction. David begins by lamenting the fact that the ark of the covenant (the only artifact that resides in the Most Holy Place) is housed in the lowly tabernacle. At this point in Israel's history, they do not yet have a permanent building like a temple. Thus, David feels pity for God's dwelling place: "See now, I dwell in a house of cedar, but the ark of God dwells in a tent" (2 Sam 7:2).

The way God responds might appear rude:

> Thus says the Lord: Would you build me a house to dwell in? I have not lived in a house since the day I brought up the people of Israel from Egypt to this day, but I have been moving about in a tent for my dwelling. In all places where I have moved with all the people of Israel, did I speak a word with any of the judges of Israel, whom I commanded to shepherd my people Israel, saying, "Why have you not built me a house of cedar?" (2 Sam 7:5b–7)

In situations between humans, we might politely say, "No, thank you," or express gratitude for a thoughtful gesture. What is more, God reminds David of David's humble origins: "I took you from the pasture, from following the sheep" (2 Sam 7:8). God's response might appear off-putting but is very fitting when we remember that he is the independent Creator. In other words, God is saying that he has no need for anything. As much as David's desire to build God a temple is sincere, it neglects the spiritual reality: God is independent and has no need for anything outside himself. Accordingly, God has to remind David that God is the one who has provided everything for David (2 Sam 7:8–9). David is merely a passive recipient of God's bountiful generosity.

It is in this context of God asserting his sovereignty that he establishes the Davidic covenant. Thus, in the covenants that God establishes in Scripture, God first reminds his people that he alone is sovereign and that the covenants are not made based on them or their potential. Every covenant is an expression of God's sheer grace and based on his own character and promises.

With the centrality of God in mind, we can now reflect upon how the Davidic covenant is a development of God's previous promises and covenants.

Christ as the True David

"Forever" Reign

One of the key promises of the Davidic covenant is victory over Israel's enemies:

> And I will appoint a place for my people Israel and will plant them, so that they may dwell in their own place and be disturbed no more. And violent men shall afflict them no more, as formerly, from the time that I appointed judges over my people Israel. And I will give you rest from all your enemies. (2 Sam 7:10–11)

This promise is meaningful when we think about Israel's history. Israel begins as a nation that is subjugated by Egypt. Even after the deliverance from Egypt, Israel is vulnerable to other peoples who are stronger. All along, God provides military victories that are humanly impossible. This is most evident in Judges where God raises various individuals to deliver Israel from foreign oppression. But all these victories and deliverances are temporary. After a period of peace, Israel relapses into their idolatrous ways, which begins another cycle of oppression.[15]

In the Davidic covenant, God promises victory over Israel's enemies that is "forever":

> I will establish the throne of his kingdom *forever*. . . . And your house and your kingdom shall be made sure *forever* before me. Your throne shall be established *forever*. (2 Sam 7:13b, 16)

The word is from the Hebrew *'olam*, and it is repeated three times (2 Sam 7:13, 16 [x2]).[16] This permanence is supplemented by the verb "establish," which is from the Hebrew *kun* (2 Sam 7:12, 13, 16).[17]

God is therefore clarifying the decisive victory that is originally promised to Adam and Eve:

---

15. Since the redemption of Christ is the ultimate story, there are many mini-redemptions that are temporary or limited in scope, especially in the Old Testament (Poythress, *In the Beginning*, 209–18).

16. The primary glosses from the *DCH* are "everlastingness, eternity, ancient time, long duration" (*DCH*, s.v. "עוֹלָם," 6:300–307); from *HALOT*, "long time, duration (usually eternal, eternity, but not in a philosophical sense)" (*HALOT*, s.v. "עוֹלָם," #6867).

17. The primary glosses from the *DCH* are "be firm, be secure, be ready, be lasting" (*DCH*, s.v. "כון," 4:373–76); from *HALOT*, "be established" or "be steadfast, be sure" (*HALOT*, s.v. "כון," #4184).

> I will put enmity between you and the woman,
>> and between your offspring and her offspring;
> he shall bruise your head,
>> and you shall bruise his heel.
> (Gen 3:15)

At the time of Gen 3, how this promise unfolds is vague. Adam and Eve even think that the "offspring" might be Cain! When we get to Abraham (Gen 12:1–3), we learn that this offspring will come specifically from his line and will be more of a blessing than a warrior. When we get to Moses, we learn that this offspring will be regarded as a firstborn son who has more of a priestly function. Now with the Davidic covenant, the description of this offspring stresses kingly qualities. What is emphasized is the offspring's permanent reign (2 Sam 7:12–13). So the promised offspring of Gen 3:15 is not generically from the line of Adam, Abraham, or Israel, but specifically from David, which we later see zeroes in on Jesus Christ. Only Christ embodies all the qualities hinted through these promises of being a warrior, a blessing, a firstborn, a priest, and a king.

Sonship and Kingdom

Two other promises of the Davidic covenant also clarify what God has promised before: sonship and kingdom.

> When your days are fulfilled and you lie down with your fathers, *I will raise up your offspring after you, who shall come from your body*, and **I will establish his kingdom**. He shall build a house for my name, and **I will establish the throne of his kingdom forever**. I will be to him a father, and he shall be to me a son. (2 Sam 7:12–14a)

The *italicized* text shows that God will be a father to one of his offsprings. The **bold** text highlights the offspring will have a kingdom. As we saw in chapters 1 and 3, sonship and kingdom are also combined in Adam and the Mosaic covenant. Adam is created in the image of God (Gen 1:26–27), which implies a parent-child relational dynamic (Gen 5:1–3), and he is given dominion over all of God's creation (Gen 1:26, 28–30; 2:19–20). Likewise, Israel is regarded as God's firstborn (Exod 4:22–23; see also Exod 11–13) and then later given the identity as a "kingdom of priests" (Exod 19:6). Part of God's promise has always been for someone to be (1) a son to God and (2) a king for God's people. Hence, the Davidic covenant is not entirely new or a replacement of previous promises. Rather, the Davidic covenant crystallizes these earlier promises.

Sadly, the history of Israel's kingship is largely a failure. King after king, they are wicked and lead the people astray. God, in his steadfast love, still provides for Israel, especially prophets who are designated to lead these kings into repentance. Yet these kings persist in their idolatry, even killing some of the prophets (e.g., 1 Kgs 18:4, 2 Ch 24:20–21, Jer 26:20–23). Reading this portion of Scripture (1–2 Kings, 1–2 Chronicles) through the narrative diagram and the covenantal-iterative flow magnifies the sin of Israel. Yet the sin of Israel cannot outlast the patience of God. God is still trustworthy to fulfill all his promises and covenants despite his people.

But the fulfillment does not take place until the New Testament. This is why Paul later writes, "All the promises of God find their Yes in [Christ]" (2 Cor 1:20a). Only Christ is the one who establishes the forever kingdom and is the perfectly obedient Son of God. Only his death and resurrection can *both* pay for the consequences of the sin *and* accomplish the requirements of God. While Israel's history had only a few righteous kings, whose reign only lasts decades, Christ is the eternal king whose reign is forever. Therefore, his subjects can rest securely and flourish in his righteous rule— not just for a generation but for all of eternity!

DAVID WITHIN THE APPROACH

As we can see, David, like every other part of reality, is merely a window into God's character and promises. Sadly, we lionize David, propping him up as the main character to emulate. When we do this, we not only fail to read Scripture as intended, but we do not see how all these are ultimately about Christ.

Space does not permit us to apply this approach to all the passages about David, but if we were to, then we will see David as intended: a side character just like Abraham, Moses, Israel, and others. What emerges is a glorious view of God, not David. God is the one who is true to his character and faithful with his promises. With God as the main character, we can recognize patterns in Scripture that would be otherwise difficult to notice.

In terms of patterns prior to David, David offers a glimpse of how Adam should have wielded his authority or how Israel should have embodied their priestly-kingly identity. In terms of patterns after David, David deepens our longing for the True David. The Problem of Sin sheds light on David's shortcomings so that we can see our own. While David has his heroic moments, inconsistency permeates his life. Thus, it is not just David's epic failure with Bathsheba (2 Sam 11–12) but the way he lies to the priests and Achish, resulting in the deaths of priests (1 Sam 21–22); how he joins the Philistines and becomes a man of violence (1 Sam 27); how he passively neglects the duties of a father by not disciplining his son Amnon when Amnon rapes David's daughter Tamar (2 Sam 13); how he accumulates multiple wives even though this is explicitly prohibited in the Torah (2 Sam 5:13; cf. Deut 17:17); and so on. In this way, David fits the pattern that we see earlier in Adam and Israel: God grants the side characters precious blessings—whether the image of God, deliverance from Egypt as a firstborn, or kingship and the Davidic covenant—only for them to be spurned.

But David's confidence is not ultimately in himself, but in God. His repentance for committing adultery with Bathsheba and murdering her husband is representative: "Have mercy on me, O God, *according to your steadfast love; according to your abundant mercy* blot out my transgressions" (Ps 51:1). The apostles later regard David as a "prophet" (Acts 2:29–33) because he anticipates that the entirety of his life would be hidden behind Christ's blood (satisfying the consequences of sin) and righteousness (satisfying the requirements of God).

Christ is therefore the True David. Christ alone is the perfectly righteous king whose reign endures forever, establishing rest and peace for all his subjects. Christ is the offspring that is vaguely promised in Gen 3:15 to destroy the ultimate serpent, the true Goliath. Christ does not merely trust and submit to the Father during the highlights of his life, but consistently and flawlessly in every other aspect. Christ, who knew no sin or iniquity, was disciplined for the iniquity of his people through his death (2 Cor 5:21, 2 Sam 7:14–15). Therefore it is through the death and resurrection of Christ that he secures for his people the "steadfast love" of God promised in the Davidic covenant (2 Sam 7:15).

SUMMARY

Like *Joker* or *Maleficent*, Scripture contains origin stories that provide fascinating perspectives on the background of various individuals. Unlike these movies, however, we are given a glimpse not of the character of David, Moses, Abraham, or others, but of God himself. Thus, David's origin story does not go back merely to his father, Jesse, or grandfather, Obed, or even to Judah. Nor does his origin story begin with the identity and blessings lavished upon Israel or Adam. Instead, like all of reality, David's origin story provides a glimpse into God's character and promises. Though David's life and lineage are full of shame, God maintains it precisely the way his sovereign will intends so that it can usher in the True David. As we have seen, every road of Scripture not only leads to but is grounded, saturated, and culminating in Christ alone! As Scripture repeatedly sears this simple truth into our hearts and minds, it eventually spills into the way we see every road of life.

QUESTIONS FOR REFLECTION AND PRAYER

a. Throughout this book, we have seen that the characters of the Old Testament function as spiritual mirrors to us. How can you relate with some of these characters (e.g., Adam and Eve, Moses and Israel, Tamar and Judah, Rahab and Achan, Ruth and Naomi, David)?

b. Another theme that emerges in Scripture is that God is faithful to his promises *despite* his people. Not only is God the main character, but often the side characters (including us) act like the antagonists!

  1. How have you experienced this in your own life?
  2. How does this deepen your appreciation for the death and resurrection of Christ?

c. God continually chooses those who are overlooked by human standards while those who are expected to be righteous are often negative examples. The key factor is a humble trust and submission to God's character and promises, which are exemplified perfectly in Christ.

  1. Take a moment to praise God that this humble trust and submission are already credited to you through the resurrection of Christ.
  2. How is the Spirit conforming you to grow in this trust and submission?

d. Try applying the narrative diagram to one or all of the following passages: 1 Sam 21:1–9 (22:6–23); 1 Sam 21:10–15; 1 Sam 24; 2 Sam 11; 2 Sam 13.

5

Christ as the Epitome of All Examples

Good inside jokes can be either enjoyable and nostalgic or frustrating and alienating. The difference is whether we are aware of the backstory of the joke. If we are unaware, then hearing one inside joke after another can be tiresome. Not knowing when or what the punch line is, we feel pressured to laugh during certain social cues. In many ways, this reflects the way we engage with Scripture. We know that we should cherish it—sometimes we might even feel pressured to look the part. Without understanding the backstory, however, our engagement with God's word eventually becomes frustrating and even alienating, which has direct implications for the way we see the gospel, our relationship with God, and life in general.

Now that we are on the New Testament, it is important to understand that it is like a series of good inside jokes. Without an awareness of the underlying backstories, we do not really understand the jokes. This is particularly true because the New Testament reveals Jesus Christ in the context of the Old Testament. This implies that readers are sufficiently familiar with the Old Testament so that they recognize the similarities between Jesus and other figures, such as Adam, Israel, and David. Thus, intertextuality is crucial to help us appreciate who Christ is and what he has done.[1]

More importantly, the New Testament also reveals Christ to be different from the figures of the Old Testament. Everything in the Old Testament

---

1. On this topic in the form of a commentary, see Beale and Carson, *Commentary on the New Testament*.

is merely shadows of Christ.² Therefore, Jesus is not merely one example among many but is distinct in significant ways. The bulk of this chapter shows how Christ is the epitome of all examples. This chapter also explains the principles of intertextuality so that we can apply it ourselves.

We begin with a brief summary of what has transpired in Scripture since chapter 4 and a reflection upon the threefold approach in light of Christ.

SETTING UP THE BIRTH OF CHRIST (2 SAMUEL TO MALACHI)

This section provides a summary of what has transpired in Scripture since chapter 4 and a sample of how to apply the approach. Since we are dealing with many books of the Old Testament, we summarize them as eras rather than passages:

Era	Indicatives	Imperatives	Fulfillment
Monarchy (2 Sam–2 Chr; various Prophets)	God establishes the kingdom of Israel through military victories; provides kings, priests, and prophets to remind them of their relationship with God; blesses them with a majestic temple so that they can enjoy God's presence; etc.	Israel to trust in God and enjoy his presence so that they can fulfill their identity as his firstborn and be a blessing to the world.	Israel repeatedly falls into idolatry; places their hope in foreign alliances; rejects/kills the prophets; carves idolatrous images in the temple; etc. These result in their exile.
Exile (Esther; various Prophets)	Despite rejecting God's word and being in exile, God reveals words of hope; enables Israel to experience his presence and favor; promises the new covenant; reassures them that the exile is out of disciplinary love and only temporary; etc.	Israel to learn repentance and wait upon the Lord.	Israel is generally faithful to God during this time (e.g., Daniel, Esther, Nehemiah).

2. Another way of describing this relation is the ectype and archetype.

Era	Indicatives	Imperatives	Fulfillment
Return (Ezra–Nehemiah; various Prophets)	God stirs the Persian ruler, Cyrus, to release Israel from exile; provides Israel with resources to rebuild Jerusalem and the temple; renews all the promises that he has made with Israel; etc.	Israel to learn from the exile and renew their trust in God.	Israel loses motivation to rebuild Jerusalem; desecrates the sacrificial system; violates many of the laws (e.g., Sabbath); etc.[3]

Although this table does not do justice to the range and richness of the Old Testament, it does help us see patterns. For instance, God blesses his people with a royal identity (*monarchy*), but his people squander such blessings, leading them to *exile*; yet God graciously brings his people back through a *return* because of his steadfast love. This same sequence is present in other portions of Scripture:[4]

Era	Adam	Israel	David
Monarchy	Adam is created in the image of God and given dominion/authority over all God's precious creation.	Israel is a royal priesthood and a kingdom of priests.	Though an overlooked shepherd boy and the eighth son of Jesse, he is anointed as king and is blessed with many military victories.

---

3. This table does not include the wisdom literature or the Writings (i.e., Job, Psalms, Proverbs, Ecclesiastes, Song of Solomon), though some of the Psalms would fit in these eras. For an introduction on how this approach can be applied to the Writings, refer to the appendix.

4. In each of these examples, there is a kingly, prophetic, and priestly role, which are the three main offices of the Old Testament that are all fulfilled in Christ. We already saw Adam's priestly role (Gen 2:15), but he also has a prophetic one since he is responsible for relaying God's law to Eve (Gen 2:16–17; cf. Gen 3:5). God also gives Israel priestly and prophetic roles by virtue of receiving the tabernacle and law. David is king but has prophetic qualities: As a king, his primary responsibility is to be intimate with the law, he wrote many of the Psalms, and he is later labelled a prophet by Peter (Acts 2:30). Regarding his priestly qualities, it is his reign that sets up the establishment of the temple, and throughout his own life and psalms, he values priestly symbols (e.g., 2 Sam 6, Ps 110:4).

Era	Adam	Israel	David
Exile	Adam neglects his kingly privileges: he submits to the lies of the serpent while rejecting God. This results in the exile from the garden.	Rather than living according to their new identity, they rebel against God repeatedly. This results in the wandering in the wilderness.	His egregious sin against Bathsheba and Uriah results in a dysfunctional family dynamic, leading him to flee from his son Absalom.
Return	God nonetheless offers a promise for a return through his posterity.	God nonetheless delivers Israel into the promised land.	God brings David back to the throne and establishes the Davidic covenant.

The purpose of these tables and patterns is to cement further that God alone is the main character and that his trustworthiness persists despite countless examples of sin. This is the necessary backstory for Jesus Christ. But before unpacking these inside jokes, let's revisit the threefold approach in light of Christ.

THE APPROACH IN LIGHT OF CHRIST

Throughout this book, we have been applying the threefold approach: the CREATOR-creature Distinction, the Problem of Sin, and the Organism of Scripture.

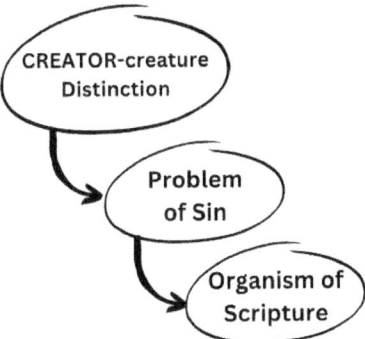

Because of who Christ is—namely, being fully God and human, and without sin—each concept must be reconsidered.

The Creator-Creature Distinction

Although Christ is fully human and fully divine, it is still useful to factor in the Creator-creature Distinction because it helps us appreciate how glorious he is as a human and how humble he is as God. Thus, we can see the original diagram modified slightly:[5]

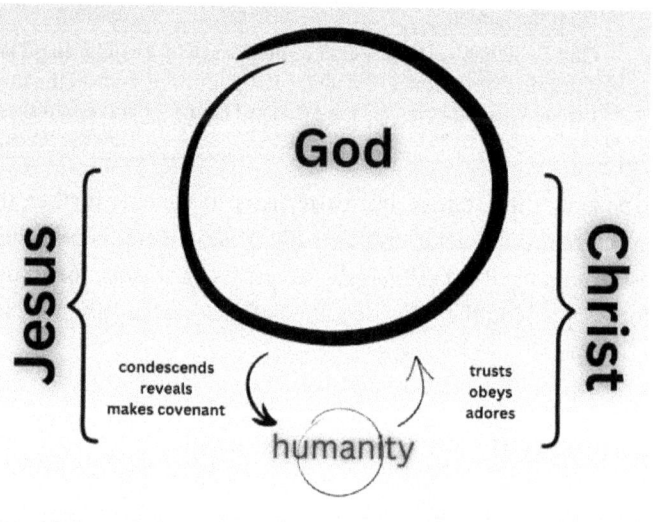

On the one hand, if the Old Testament teaches us to appreciate the ways in which God condescends, reveals, and covenants, then Jesus elevates all these in unimaginable ways. Christ lowers himself to become his own creation (*condescends*) in order to express the glories of God in the most concrete way (*reveals*) so that he can establish the new covenant (*covenants*; Jer 31:31–34, Ezek 36:26–27).[6]

On the other hand, if the Old Testament shows the inconsistent ways in which humans trust, obey, and adore God, then Jesus fulfills these with perfection. Despite facing more difficult circumstances, Christ faithfully submits to the Father with joy—even suffering death on a cross (Phil 2:6–8)! Thus, he not only pays for the consequences of the sins of his people, but actively satisfies the requirements of God that his people did not meet.

---

5. It is inappropriate to refer to Jesus as a "creature," so the diagram uses the labels of "God" and "humanity."

6. As Calvin writes, Jesus "deigns to make us one with him." *Institutes*, 3.11.10.

Christ as the Epitome of All Examples

In Christ, we therefore marvel at the inconceivable extent to which God condescends, reveals, and covenants while marveling at the extent to which a human can fulfill perfect righteousness through trust, obedience, and adoration.

The Problem of Sin

The Gospels emphasize that Christ is flawless in his trust in the Father and is therefore without sin, which is made explicit in the Epistles (2 Cor 5:21a, 1 John 3:5). So while the Old Testament is replete with disappointing outcomes and failed fulfillments, Christ repeatedly proves his perfect righteousness and therefore overcomes the Problem of Sin.

However, this does not mean that Christ is not tempted in every way (Heb 4:15). Everyone who comes in contact with Christ is enslaved to the Problem of Sin. The prologue to John makes this clear. His own creation, rather than embracing the source of life and its Creator, actually rejects him (John 1:11). If the Old Testament contains examples of people distorting, suppressing, and rejecting God's character and promises, then the Gospels take this to another level. Even Jesus's family and disciples fail to recognize who he is, despite being the radiance of God's glory (Col 1:15, Heb 1:3)! Moreover, his environment and circumstances are much more difficult than what anybody endured in the Old Testament. Yet despite being surrounded by sinners in a world broken by sin, Christ proves to be perfectly righteous.

The Organism of Scripture

As mentioned in chapter 2, there is a literary flow within the Organism of Scripture: the Gospels show not only how Christ fulfills the Torah (the first figure below) but how all of Scripture (and reality) orbit around Christ and not the Torah (the second and third figures). This is because Christ is the embodiment of the Torah. In chapter 3, we mentioned that the Ten Commandments are introduced as the "Ten Words" (Exod 20:1, 24:3–4). The New Testament calls Jesus *the* Word (John 1:1).

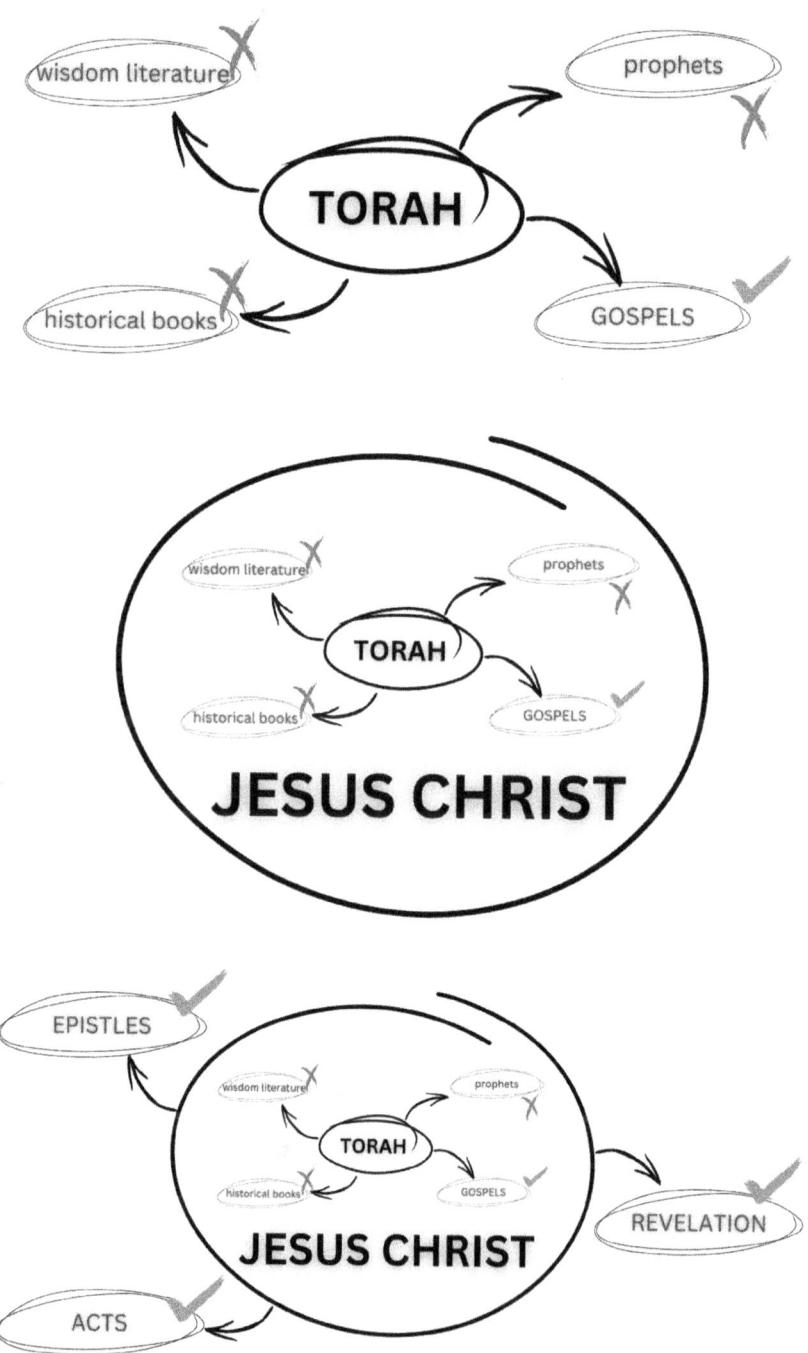

We can also see Christ in the light of the covenantal/iterative flow. Throughout the Old Testament, there are countless failed indicative-imperative-fulfillment triads. God withholds his wrath and extends mercy by wrapping each of these failures around another triad iteratively, much like a Russian doll set. Finally, in the Gospels there is a sigh of relief because Christ breaks this demoralizing pattern. He actively fulfills every imperative with his perfect life (satisfying the requirements of God) and addresses all the failed imperatives (paying the consequences of the sins of his people). His death absolves his people from the wrath that should be afflicted on them while his resurrection imputes to his people the righteousness that he fulfilled, which is also the template to which his people are inevitably conformed because of the Holy Spirit.

Diagram and Table

In this chapter, we mainly reflect upon the Gospels, which are mostly narrative. Although we can use the same narrative diagram introduced in chapter 2, it is better to adjust it slightly because of who Jesus is. Earlier we saw how Adam, Moses, and David are all side characters and that God is the main character. But Christ is both the main and side character. He simultaneously represents what the ideal human is (i.e., he is 100 percent human) and what God is like (i.e., he is 100 percent divine).

As depicted in the diagram, the key differences are grayed and emboldened/enlarged:

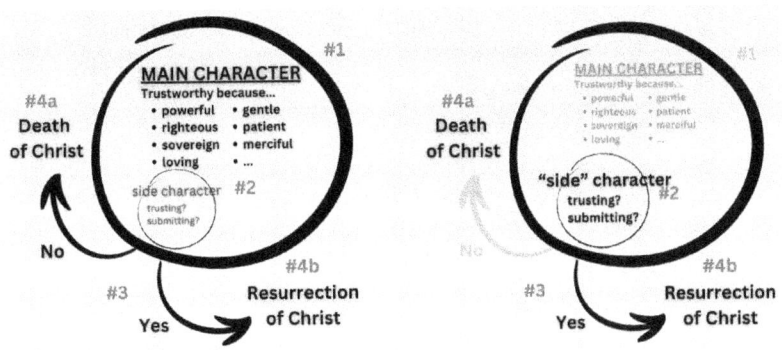

The two key differences are: (a) for #1, we do not get as much explicit details of God the Father (so the "side" character part is emboldened/enlarged), and (b) Jesus never fails, so #4a never occurs—yet he nonetheless dies for the sins of his people.

There is therefore a shift from the Old Testament to the Gospels. In the Old Testament, the continual failures of the side characters provide more background for the sin that Christ addresses (#4a), but the significance of examples of obedience (#4b) is not as obvious. In the Gospels, the perfect obedience of Christ provides more background for his righteousness (#4b). This is supremely relevant because, as we saw in chapter 2, his righteousness has at least the following implications:

1. It is the epitome of all examples of righteousness, including the ones from the Old Testament.
2. It is necessary for the efficacy of his death (paying for the consequences of our sin).
3. It is imputed to his people (officially and legally declared by the Father—satisfying the requirements of God).
4. It is that to which we are being conformed (progressively and gradually transformed by the Spirit).

Each of these implications is profound. It takes the entirety of the New Testament to unpack and a full lifetime to experience each of them! Thus, the table below is a summary of the diagram and how narratives about Jesus can be applied to make all this more accessible:

#1	**Main Character's Trustworthiness:** In the Gospels, there are not as many details about God the Father. Most of the attention is given to Jesus. In this way, he is both the main and side character.	Indicative
#2	**Main Character's Invitation:** What makes Jesus's life perfectly righteous is his trust and submission to the Father. Often we get fixated on his miracles, wisdom, or details about his life. But the fundamental reason for his perfect righteousness is his trust and submission.	Imperative
#3	**Side Character's Response:** Despite living in a world that is broken by sin with people who sin against him, Christ always obeys the Father out of his trust and submission.	Fulfillment

#4	**Christ's Fulfillment:**	
	Every example of Christ's obedience is necessary for our salvation. His perfect life is required for the efficacy of his death and fulfills all righteousness that is imputed to us through his resurrection. Among other things, his resurrection declares his life to be righteous and that his death is unjust. Thus, the resurrection makes the example of his righteousness found in the passage relevant in at least the following ways:	**Fulfillment**
	a. It offers a behind-the-scenes perspective into why we can trust in the power of his death so that the consequences of our sin can be addressed.	
	b. It is legally and officially declared to be ours by the Father through the resurrection, satisfying the requirements of God.	
	c. It is what the Spirit is gradually and progressively transforming us to embody.	

The diagram and table above are a great starting point for a majority of the narratives about Jesus.

Now, the purpose of the following sections is to present examples of three inside jokes that revisit what we saw in the previous chapters of Adam, Israel, and David. We now meet the True Adam, True Israel, and True David.

CHRIST AS THE TRUE ADAM

We earlier saw how God introduces himself in the opening chapters of Scripture. Although he is the independent CREATOR, he lovingly creates all of reality so that humanity can flourish. Only humans are created in the image of God and are therefore lavished with a plethora of blessings: Adam is privileged with a partnership with God, a glorious role and purpose, dominion over the rest of God's creation, and "laws" that are a window into God's generous character and promises. Because of Adam's unique role as federal head, as he trusts and submits to God, every aspect of creation blossoms. Adam instead distorts, suppresses, and rejects God's character and promises, so every aspect of creation falls into the decay of sin, introducing death and other destructive symptoms.

In the face of humanity's rebellion, God nonetheless promises vindication. As the story of Scripture unfolds, a desperate longing for a new Adam who can destroy the serpent mounts. Sure, there might have been glimpses or examples of what this new Adam might look like: despite humanity's rebellion against the Cultural Mandate (i.e., the Tower of Babel), God raises up Abram; despite Egypt's oppressive slavery over God's promised people, God raises up Moses; and despite the giant defier of God's character (i.e., Goliath), God raises up David. But in the end they all fall short, accentuating the dire need for the True Adam. It is in the context of this miserable state of humanity and of God's gracious promise that the New Testament introduces Jesus.

This section shows only one portrayal of the True Adam, primarily through the opening chapters of the Gospel of Luke.[7] Although it can be tempting to rush into the connections with old Adam, it is crucial first to have a good sense of the base passage. So read Luke 4:1–13 on your own before proceeding.

Basic Summary of Jesus's Temptation

As a simple summary, Jesus has just been baptized (Luke 3:21–22) where he has heard the voice from God the Father: "You are my beloved son; with you I am well pleased" (Luke 3:22). Immediately after this verse, Luke unexpectedly provides a genealogy that connects Jesus to Adam (Luke 3:23–38). And then immediately after the genealogy, we are treated with Jesus's encounter with the devil (Luke 4:1–13).

The setting of this encounter emphasizes Jesus's vulnerability: not only is he in the hostile wilderness, but he has been fasting forty days in complete isolation (Luke 4:2). It is in this state of vulnerability that Jesus faces temptations from the devil. The heart of the temptations is to undermine God's character and promises. Nevertheless, Jesus withstands the devil and his temptations.

Backstory of Jesus's Temptation and Similarities

The more we know about the base passage, the more we can identify the backstory and similarities. As summarized above, there are a few details in the base passage that evoke earlier passages.[8] Notice the similarities in the

---

7. For a fuller treatment, see Crowe, *Last Adam*.

8. The primary ways of finding intertextual connections to other passages are cross-references and grammatical and thematic similarities. For a detailed treatment, see Beale, *Handbook on the New Testament*.

table below that show how Luke is setting up an inside joke by portraying Jesus as the True Adam:[9]

Jesus Christ	Similarity	Adam
Luke 3:22: "You are my beloved son; with you I am well pleased."	God Blesses the Adamic Figure (indicative)	Adam is created in the image of God with many blessings (Gen 1:26–30; 2:9, 15–23; etc.).
	God Speaks to the Adamic Figure (imperative)	"You may surely eat of every tree of the garden, but of the tree of the knowledge of good and evil you shall not eat, for in the day that you eat of it you shall surely die" (Gen 2:16b–17).
Luke 3:23–28: Establishing connection between the two Adams through a genealogy (Gen 5:1–32)		
Luke 4:1–13: The temptation by the devil.	The Adamic Figure Is Tempted (fulfillment)	Temptation by the serpent (Gen 3:1–7).

Luke 3:21–22: God Blesses the Adamic Figure (Indicative)

Before we see either Adamic figure in action, Scripture emphasizes the blessings bestowed by God. We already mentioned the rich blessings God bestows upon Adam. For the True Adam, God the Father affirms his love and reminds him of his true identity as the "beloved son." All this is punctuated by the Holy Spirit descending upon Jesus (Luke 3:21–22). Applying the covenantal/iterative flow, these blessings are the indicatives.

Luke 3:21–22: God Speaks to the Adamic Figure (Imperative)

The other similarity is that God speaks to both Adamic figures before each of them is tempted. In chapter 1, we noted that God issues a clear prohibition, which is a reminder of God's generous character and promises (Gen 2:16b–17). God is being clear in this prohibition, not because he is strict but so that Adam is equipped to detect the lies of temptation.

As I explain further below, God's speech to Jesus is also a significant part of his temptation. The last thing Jesus hears before fasting forty days

---

9. Luke is also portraying Jesus as the True Israel in this temptation, but space does not allow us to explore this connection.

and hearing the lies of the devil is, "You are my beloved son; with you I am well pleased" (Luke 3:22).

Following the covenantal/iterative flow, God's speech is the imperative. How can each Adamic figure live according to what God has said? On the surface, it is as simple as Adam not eating from that one tree. Although this is true, this book's approach helps us see that the underlying issue is one of trust. Adam is called to trust in God's character and promises—every time Adam does not eat from that tree, he is reminded of God's generosity and that God is worthy of his submission.

In this way, we see more clearly the connection with Jesus. For Jesus, there is of course no tree from which he needs to refrain. Instead, Jesus is also called to trust God's character and promises—will Jesus trust and submit to the fact that he is the beloved son of the Father? We will see that in each of the roles that Jesus fulfills—the True Adam, the True Israel, and the True David—the underlying identity is that of a son.

Luke 3:23–38: Connection via Genealogy

After Jesus's baptism, Luke inserts Jesus's genealogy. Why would Luke place the genealogy at this point in his Gospel? Chronologically it is odd, but it makes sense when we recognize that Luke is depicting Jesus as the True Adam. Hence, Luke's genealogy traces Jesus back to Seth and Adam.[10] Before we see Jesus being tempted, Luke wants us first to envision Jesus as the True Adam. This is a signal that the promised offspring of Eve (Gen 3:15) has "entered the chat."[11]

Luke 4:1–13: The Adamic Figure Is Tempted (Fulfillment)

Once Luke establishes Jesus's connection with Adam, we can finally peer into the first anticipated showdown between the promised offspring of Eve and the offspring of the serpent (Gen 3:15). The devil hurls three

---

10. This contrasts with Matthew's genealogy, which goes back to David and Abraham (Matt 1:1–17). For commentary on the differences between the two genealogies, see Luz, *Matthew*, 75; Bovon, *Luke 1*, 133–36.

11. Hence, the names in Luke's genealogy (Luke 3:36b–38) match the names of Gen 5:1–32. The differences are that of spelling, probably because Luke is using the Greek translation of the Old Testament, e.g., Mahalaleel versus Mahalalel, and Enos versus Enosh.

temptations, each of which has the same tactic that we noticed earlier: to distort, suppress, and/or reject God's character or promises.

The last thing that Jesus heard is a revelation of God's character and promises: "*You are my beloved Son*; with you I am well pleased" (Luke 3:22). In this short line, God reveals his character of fatherhood to Jesus and his promise of his pleasure with him. As indicated in both *italicized* texts, it is this truth, which is tied to God's character and promises, that the devil attacks: "*If you are the Son of God*, command this stone to become bread" (Luke 4:3). The other two temptations use the same strategy to distort, suppress, and/or reject God's character or promises (Luke 4:6, 9–11). Hence, Jesus's temptation is fundamentally the same as Adam and Eve's. The table below shows the specific revelation of God (left column) that is being challenged in the temptation (right column):

God's Character and Promises	The Temptation
"You are my beloved son; with you I am well pleased" (Luke 3:22).	"*If you are the Son of God . . .*" (Luke 4:3, 9).
"*You may surely eat of every tree of the garden*, but of the tree of the knowledge of good and evil you shall not eat, for in the day that you eat of it **you shall surely die**" (Gen 2:16b–17).	"Did God actually say, '*You shall not eat of any tree in the garden*'? . . . **You will not surely die**" (Gen 3:1b, 4b)

What is at stake in temptations is not a specific tree, action, behavior, or speech—these are mere symptoms that often mask the essence of sin. Sin is far more foundational and destructive. What is at stake is a distrust of God's character and promises. In the light of the surplus of God's gracious indicatives, he is calling us simply to trust him. Once that trust erodes into a distortion, suppression, and/or rejection, then the gates are open wide for sin and its destructive symptoms (e.g., actions, behaviors, and speech).

Differences of Jesus's Temptation

Now that we have a sufficient understanding of the base passage and its backstory and similarities, we can identify the differences. Although similarities are fascinating and the prerequisite to identifying the differences, what is most significant are the differences. The differences tell something unique about Jesus. They are akin to the joke's punch line.

The Setting

The most obvious difference is that the setting of Jesus's temptation could not be more adverse, while the setting of Adam's temptation could not be more ideal. While Jesus is in the wilderness (Luke 4:1), has been fasting forty days (Luke 4:2), and is in solitude (he has not heard anything since the baptism, Luke 3:22), Adam enjoys the lush garden of Eden, has access to all sorts of succulent and nourishing foods, and is blessed with the companionship of Eve.

The Trust

Despite the vulnerability of Jesus and the guile of the temptations, the True Adam prevails because of his unwavering trust in God's character and promises. Scripture is Jesus's weapon of choice.[12] More importantly, the True Adam understands Scripture as intended. This is one of the fundamental differences between not only Christ and Adam, but Christ and everyone else. Christ is the epitome, and everyone else is merely examples who foreshadow him. Adam, Eve, and the rest of the people of God distort, suppress, and eventually reject the revelation of God. They fixate on the imperatives while ignoring the indicatives, or they see themselves as the main character rather than God, or they fail to see God's revelation as a window into his character and promises. Christ, however, not only cherishes and understands God and his word as intended but perfectly trusts and submits.

The Outcome

The serpent only needed one temptation for Adam and Eve, whereas Jesus withstands the devil even after a series of temptations. Throughout Scripture, everyone is generally "light work" for Satan. Satan uses the same tactic, and for the most part it works. In these temptations, however, Satan recognizes that Jesus is "built different." This is why the devil quotes an obscure portion of Scripture in the last temptation (Luke 4:11 / Ps 91:12):

> On their hands they will bear you up,
>   lest you strike your **foot** against a stone.

---

12. Jesus intentionally quotes Deuteronomy to show that he is also True Israel (Luke 4:4, 8, and 12).

The emboldened word, **foot**, suggests what the devil might be thinking. The "foot" has special significance for the devil. The original promise means that although the serpent's offspring bruises the "heel" of Eve's offspring, the serpent's offspring receives the fatal strike to the head (Gen 3:15). The devil is not only sizing up Jesus but is wondering if he is Eve's promised offspring. This connection is clearer when we look at the double emphasis on serpent (see *italicized* below—*adder* is basically a *serpent*) in the verse that comes after what the devil quotes (Ps 91:13):

> You will tread on the lion and the *adder*;
> the young lion and the *serpent* you will trample underfoot.

As Jesus refutes each temptation, the devil panics: "Is he Eve's promised offspring who will destroy me?"

Biblical Principles and Practical Implications

Now that we have a general sense of the base passage, the backstory, and the similarities and differences, we are now ready to understand the biblical principles. What does all this say about God's character and promises? How might this enrich our appreciation for the death and resurrection of Christ? And what implications do all these have for the people of Christ?

As inspirational as Jesus is, it is not meant for us only to marvel and think, "Gee, Jesus was a great guy," "I can never do that," or "I guess I should try to be better." To understand the significance of Jesus's life, we turned to the New Testament Epistles that teach us that he secured these blessings *for us* (e.g., Rom 4:25, 5:12–21).[13]

Since Adam functions as a federal head, his actions have a cascading effect on all that he represents, especially the rest of humanity. Jesus, as the True Adam, also functions as a federal head. So his actions have a cascading effect on all that he represents. Accordingly, the righteousness of Christ in this passage and throughout the Gospels has the four implications explained earlier: (1) it is the epitome of other examples of righteousness; (2) it is necessary for the efficacy of Christ's death; (3) his people take credit for it; and (4) it is the script to which his people are inevitably conformed.

---

13. As a reminder, the New Testament Epistles generally contain biblical principles that explain the Gospels (and the Old Testament). This is similar to how Vos understands the Epistles as the explanation of the Gospels. Or how the Epistles are the captions to memes of the Gospels (and Old Testament). See n. 14 in chapter 2.

Thus, Jesus's role as the True Adam sheds light on a few transactions that take place, as most succinctly explained in 2 Cor 5:21: "For our sake he made him to be sin who knew no sin, so that in him we might become the righteousness of God." The table and diagram below unpack some of the meaning of this profound verse.

Text	Meaning
For our sake	Everything that Paul writes about in this verse is for our benefit (similar to Rom 4:25).
he made him to be sin	The Father regarded Jesus as sin—that is, Christ took the consequences of our sin. There are two transactions here: (1) what is implied is Adam's sin has been imputed to us (e.g., Rom 5:12–21) and (2) our sin has been imputed to Christ.
who knew no sin	To be clear, Jesus did not sin but lived in perfect righteousness, satisfying the requirements of God for his people. The perfect obedience of the entirety of his life and death is an essential part of the salvation that Christ earned for us.
so that	What is the purpose and result of Jesus's death? Paul explains in the following words.
in him	This refers to our union with Christ. Christ grafts us to himself so that we can enjoy all the benefits that he secured.
we might become the righteousness of God	One of the benefits that we enjoy because of our union with Christ is his righteousness, which brings to focus his resurrection (e.g., Rom 4:25). This, then, is the third transaction. All of Christ's perfect obedience, including his triumph over the devil in this passage, has been shared with us. This sharing is twofold: (a) the Father officially and legally declares us to have the righteousness of Christ (imputation) and (b) the Spirit gradually transforms us to embody the righteousness of Christ (conformity).

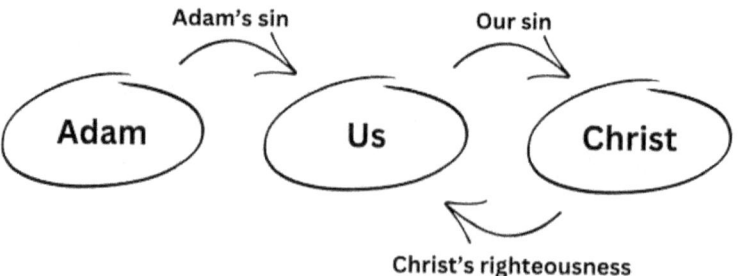

If Adam and Israel are our spiritual mirror apart from Christ, then Christ shatters that mirror and presents us with a new one! Because of his death

CHRIST AS THE EPITOME OF ALL EXAMPLES

and resurrection, our identity is no longer in old Adam but in Christ—the True Adam! Rather than being enslaved to distorting, suppressing, and rejecting God's character and promises, we are forgiven of all our sins by his death and made righteous by his resurrection!

As glorious as these truths are, this does not fully explain the importance of the True Adam or the overall majesty of Christ. We now turn to another facet of Jesus by beholding a glimpse of the True Israel.

CHRIST AS THE TRUE ISRAEL

There are many ways that the New Testament portrays Jesus as the True Israel. We will only look at one example that connects to what we saw earlier in the Mosaic covenant (chapter 3).

The Mosaic covenant blesses Israel with a new identity that is maintained as God graciously shares his presence with his people. As we saw in chapter 3, the design is the same as Adam's: as God's people enjoy his presence, they can rule and be a blessing to the rest of the world (e.g., Isa 2:2–4, Mic 4:1–3).

One of the benefits of the Mosaic covenant is the tabernacle, which later evolves into the temple. Although the tabernacle and temple have the reputation of being burdensome, this approach helps us see them rightly as God's willingness to share his presence with his people. Thus, we rightly see them as gifts.

However, because of God's holiness and the people's finitude and sin, boundaries within the tabernacle are required. Only Moses has access to the summit of the mountain, by invitation only, and he was unable to bring anyone else (Exod 24:1–2). This adumbrates the tabernacle where only the high priest is invited to the Most Holy Place.

With these parameters in mind, we can now explore the transfiguration of Jesus (Matt 17:1–8). Although there are similarities with Israel, the differences are consequential. As in the previous example, we must first comprehend the base passage. So read Matt 17:1–9 on your own before proceeding.

Basic Summary of Jesus's Transfiguration

As a brief summary, Jesus takes three disciples—Peter, James, and John—up a mountain (Matt 17:1). On the mountain, Jesus transfigures before them. His face shines like the sun, and his clothes turn white (Matt 17:2). There are other details, but an important one is that God the Father once again speaks to Jesus in the presence of witnesses. And once again, God the Father affirms Jesus's identity as son: "This is my beloved Son, with whom I am well pleased; listen to him" (Matt 17:5). The disciples respond appropriately by falling prostrate in reverence and fear (Matt 17:6).[14]

Backstory and Similarities of Jesus's Transfiguration

There is much more that can be explored in the base passage, but for now we have enough to identify the backstory and some similarities:

1. The passage begins and ends with a reference to a mountain (another example of an inclusio): going "up a high mountain" (Matt 17:1) and "coming down the mountain" (Matt 17:9). Chapter 3 established that "mountain" is repeated with emphasis in Exod 19–20.

2. God the Father speaks through a "bright cloud" (Matt 17:5). Similarly during the ratification of the Mosaic covenant, God speaks through a cloud: "Behold, I am coming to you in a thick cloud, that the people may hear when I speak with you, and may also believe you forever" (Exod 19:9). In fact, cloud is mentioned repeatedly throughout this event, often with something "bright" like lightning or fire (Exod 19:9, 16; 24:15–18).

3. Of all the people who could appear on the mountain, it is Moses and Elijah. Commentators have speculated why they are chosen. Like most things, it is probably a combination of multiple reasons: both individuals have significant encounters with God on Mount Sinai (Exod 19–40, 1 Kgs 18:8); Moses represents the Law while Elijah generally represents the Prophets—the Law and Prophets imply the fullness of Scripture; and both are regarded as prototypical prophets (Deut 18:15, Mal 4:5). At any rate, all these reasons reinforce the connection to the Mosaic covenant at Mount Sinai (Exod 19–24): it is during this event that God reveals the law by which Israel is later judged through the prophets.[15]

---

14. As Luz notes, this passage is difficult and has many meanings (*Matthew*, 395), so due to space limitations, we can only explore the ones most relevant to Christ being portrayed as the True Israel.

15. For more details, see Davies and Allison, *Saint Matthew*, 2:697–99.

These similarities indicate that the transfiguration of Jesus happened and is recorded in such a way to draw our attention to the ratification of the Mosaic covenant at Mount Sinai.[16]

Differences of Jesus's Transfiguration

The similarities above enable us not only to understand the backstory of the transfiguration but enable us to identify key differences that are telling.

Jesus's Authority

The first difference is that Jesus has full authority to go up the mountain, whereas Moses has to be invited:

Jesus Christ	Moses
"Jesus . . . led them up a high mountain by themselves" (Matt 17:1).	"And the LORD called Moses to the top of the mountain, and Moses went up" (Exod 19:20b). "Then he said to Moses, 'Come up to the LORD'" (Exod 24:1a).

As we saw in chapter 3, the reason for the boundaries are God's holiness and the finitude and sin of his people. Despite this chasm, God nonetheless makes it possible to share his presence with his people. While Moses or the high priest needs to be invited to access the summit of the mountain or the Most Holy Place, Jesus has full authority to be in the center of God's holiness.[17]

Jesus's People

The second difference is that Jesus can bring whomever to the top of the mountain. For Moses, he is warned to come by himself. Others, including the priests and elders, can go up the mountain but not to the summit (Exod

---

16. For other similarities, see Davies and Allison, *Saint Matthew*, 2:686–87.

17. This is a theme in the Old Testament that is only fulfilled by Christ (e.g., Pss 15, 24). For instance, Isa 33:14 asks who can sojourn (*gur*) to Zion (the temple of Jerusalem)? Isaiah 33:15–16 looks forward to one can actually dwell (*shakan*) in the heavenly heights (not just in Zion). How is this possible? Because he is perfectly righteous (Isa 33:15).

24:1–2). And in Moses's context, he needs to perform purification practices and offer a sacrifice (Exod 19:10–15, 24:4–8).

Jesus is not only able to bring Peter, James, and John (Matt 17:1), but there is no need for any kind of purification or sacrifice. The reason is simple: they are with Jesus. As we see in greater detail below, the Epistles explain the significance of this seemingly arbitrary detail: Christ enables us to enter not just the summit of the mountain or the physical Most Holy Place but the heavenly places, for we are cleansed by his blood (death) and clothed with his righteousness (resurrection).

Jesus's Glory

Lastly, the glory that Moses beholds is external to him because God alone is the source of glory. As Moses basks in God's presence, Moses's face radiates with God's glory. But over time, the light that reflects from Moses's face diminishes because the glory comes from God (Exod 34:29–35).

For Jesus, the brilliance comes from within himself. It does not come from the heavens or from God the Father: "And he was transfigured before them, and his face shone like the sun, and his clothes became white as light" (Matt 17:2). Jesus's glory does not fade because he himself is the source of glory.[18]

Biblical Principles and Practical Implications

So what biblical principles and practical implications can we glean from all this? Israel is given the privilege to access God's presence so that Israel can grow in their true identity (e.g., sonship, treasured possession, kingdom of priests, and holy nation). Consequently, Israel would be the vehicle through which the rest of the world experiences the redemption of God. But we saw in chapter 3 that Israel forfeits all these blessings by treating the tabernacle and temple with contempt.

If the temptation of Christ emphasizes his righteousness, the transfiguration highlights his love for God's presence and his authority to be there. This is why upon Jesus's death, the curtain dividing the Holy Place and the Most Holy place is torn (Matt 27:51; see also Heb 10:20). Hebrews

---

18. As we see in the next section, Jesus does not make use of his glory during his earthly ministry for the sake of our salvation (Phil 2:6–8). But when he returns, he will come in glory (Phil 2:9–11).

later explains that Jesus is the high priest who has access to the heavenly holy places—not merely the earthly copy of them (Heb 9:24). Paul writes that those who are in Christ are seated with him in the preeminent place of the right hand of the Father (Eph 2:6; see also 1:20–21). Those in Christ not only have access to a place that is unthinkable for Israel or even the angels, but they dwell there! Consequently, they grow in their true identity in Christ, enabling them to be the vehicle through which the rest of the world experiences the redemption of God.

How does all this take place? Predictably, Hebrews and Paul both point to the same things in the respective passages referenced above: the death and resurrection of Christ (Heb 9:23–28, Eph 2:4–5).

There are many more biblical principles and practical implications that can be harvested from Jesus being the True Israel. For now, let us turn to the final inside joke.

CHRIST AS THE TRUE DAVID

After 929 chapters of the Old Testament building suspense for Jesus, how might the New Testament finally introduce him? Through one of his famous miracles? The very first verses of the New Testament introduce Jesus through a . . . genealogy! Although a genealogy seems like a missed opportunity, it actually makes quite a few bold claims: Jesus is not only the fulfillment of the Davidic covenant, but he is the True David.[19] However, the backstories of this inside joke are even more shocking.

Before proceeding, read Matt 1:1–17 on your own. Do any of these names sound familiar? Why would the New Testament introduce Jesus this way?

The Genealogy of Christ (Matt 1:1–17)

In chapter 4, we applied the genealogy diagram to understand the context and significance of Tamar and Perez, Salmon and Rahab, and Boaz and Ruth:[20]

---

19. In fact, the first two words in the Greek (*Biblos geneseōs*) imply that Matthew is setting up a "new genesis" or "a counterpart to the story of Genesis" (Davies and Allison, *Saint Matthew*, 1:151). The genealogy also portrays Jesus as the fulfillment of the Abrahamic promise/covenant, but space does not allow us to explore this.

20. As a reminder, it is significant that women are listed (e.g., Davies and Allison,

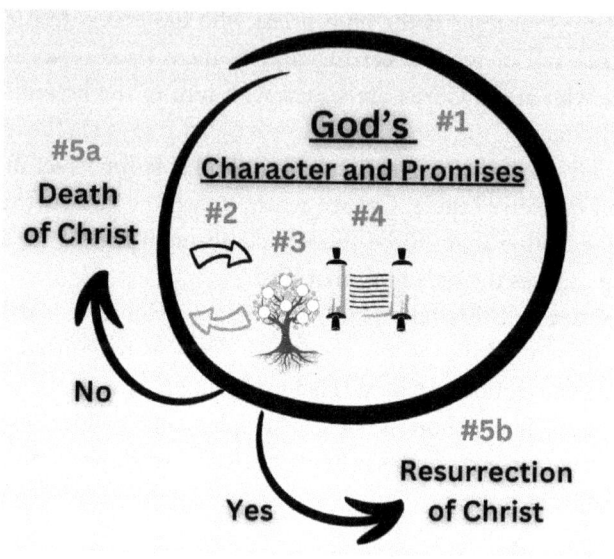

#1	Remember that genealogies, like all of Scripture and reality, are a window to God's character and promises.
#2	What comes before and after the genealogy? Does the placement of the genealogy imply anything about God's character and promises?
#3	Are there any details about any of the individuals? As much as these might be intriguing, take a step back and reflect what these details say about God. Since every human is created in the image of God, these details are ultimately a reflection of God's character.
#4	Familiarize yourself with the names. Have you seen these names before? See if there are any cross references to these names. If so, then look up their backstory (intertextuality). Their backstory is usually a narrative, so you can apply the narrative diagram.
#5	If there are negative examples from #3 or 4, then this is addressed for God's people through the death of Christ (#5a); if positive, then it foreshadows the perfect righteousness that Christ fulfills and that is imputed to his people through the resurrection of Christ (#5b).

Due to space limitations, we apply only #4 by reflecting on the most salient aspects of the kings who are mentioned in this genealogy (Matt 1:6b–11). Before viewing the table, guess how many of the following fourteen kings are considered generally faithful (shaded in gray)?

Saint Matthew, 1:170).

Christ as the Epitome of All Examples

Solomon Matt 1:7a	Despite all his wisdom and success, he egregiously violates the expectations of a king (Deut 18), which leads to his downfall (e.g., 1 Kgs 11).
Rehoboam Matt 1:7b	He foolishly obeys the advice of his peers rather than his elders, which divides the kingdom into two (1 Kgs 12-14, 2 Chr 10-12).
Abijah Matt 1:7c	He is thoroughly unfaithful (1 Kgs 15:1-8, 2 Chr 13).
Asa Matt 1:8a	He is generally faithful (1 Kgs 15:9-24, 2 Chr 14-15).
Jehosophat Matt 1:8b	He is generally faithful (1 Kgs 22:41-50, 2 Chr 20).
Joram Matt 1:8c	He is thoroughly unfaithful (2 Kgs 8:16-23, 2 Chr 21:1-7).
Uzziah Matt 1:9a	He begins faithfully but becomes arrogant and ultimately unfaithful (2 Kgs 15:1-7, 2 Chr 26).
Jotham Matt 1:9b	He is generally faithful (2 Kgs 15:32-38, 2 Chr 27).
Ahaz Matt 1:9c	He is thoroughly unfaithful (2 Kgs 16:1-4, 2 Chr 28:1-4).
Hezekiah Matt 1:10a	Bravely stands up to the Assyrians, but the ending of his life reveals his selfishness and neglect for God's kingdom and his posterity (2 Kgs 18-20, 2 Chr 29-32).
Manasseh Matt 1:10b	He is thoroughly unfaithful, even carving images of Asherah in the temple (2 Kgs 21:1-9, 2 Chr 33:1-20)!
Amon Matt 1:10c	He is thoroughly unfaithful (2 Kgs 21:19-26, 2 Chr 33:21-25).
Josiah Matt 1:11a	Discovers the Torah and executes many God-glorifying reforms, but the ending of his life reveals his arrogance (2 Kgs 22-23, 2 Chr 34-35).
Jeconiah Matt 1:11b	He is thoroughly unfaithful and represents generations of disobedient kings, so God finally sends the people into exile (2 Kgs 24:6-9, 2 Chr 36:9, Jer 22:24-30). Nevertheless, God maintains the Davidic covenant because of his own character and promises (Hag 2:23).

Only three of the kings are described as generally faithful. When combining this with David's genealogy and inconsistent life (chapter 4), a clear picture emerges. Jesus's lineage is full of shame, disobedience, and outright sin. What does this say about God's character and promises? For one, it is as Isaiah prophesied:

> He was despised and rejected by men,
>   a man of sorrows, and acquainted with grief;
> and as one from whom men hide their faces
>   he was despised, and we esteemed him not. (Isa 53:3)

Jesus is to be a man of sorrows and humility in order to empathize with those who are weak.

This is why Jesus frequently interacts with those who are shunned, like the tax collectors and prostitutes. Matthew quotes Isaiah by saying that Jesus is so gentle that he does not even break a bruised reed or quench a smoldering wick (Matt 12:20; see also Isa 42:3). Although people of authority usually abuse their roles, Jesus uses his kingship perfectly by leading those who are weak with sensitivity. He empathizes with them because such fragility is in his bloodline. This is quite contrary to those who legitimize their significance by boasting of their impeccable background.

Hence, we see that Jesus is portrayed immediately as the True David in the New Testament. However, Jesus does not wield his kingship in an arrogant or tyrannical way. Instead, Jesus's kingship is precisely how God initially envisioned it to be: one of humility and empathy.

The Victory of Christ (Gal 1:3–4, Col 2:13–15)

However, Christ does not merely empathize with the sins of his people. As the True David, Christ also conquers their wickedness. If David slays Goliath, then Christ heroically slays our sin. However, the way Christ triumphs is different and unexpected. It is, unsurprisingly, through his death and resurrection:

> Grace to you and peace from God our Father and the Lord Jesus Christ, <u>who gave himself</u> for our *sins* to **deliver** us from the present evil age, according to the will of our God and Father. (Gal 1:3–4)

> And you, who were dead in your *trespasses* and the uncircumcision of your flesh, God made alive together with him, having forgiven us all our *trespasses*, by canceling *the record of debt* that stood against us with its legal demands. This he set aside, <u>nailing it to the cross</u>. **He disarmed the rulers and authorities** and put them to open shame, **by triumphing over them** in him. (Col 2:13–15)

Christ as the Epitome of All Examples

In both these passages, the italics make it clear that *sin* is the problem being addressed (*"trespasses"* and *"debt"* are synonyms). The way that *sin* is defeated is through Jesus's <u>death</u> and resurrection, as indicated by the underlined text: "<u>who gave himself</u>" and "<u>nailing it to the cross</u>." The emboldened words refer to a military or kingly context: "**deliver**," "**disarmed the rulers and authorities**," and "**triumphing**."[21] Consequently, despite the range and depth of the sin of his people that have accrued throughout generations, his people need not worry about God's righteous wrath (e.g., Rom 3:25, Eph 2:1–7). The condemnation and consequences of their rebellion, therefore, have no power over them! Although the death and resurrection of Christ should not be separated, this provision is highlighted more in his death.

The New Testament, however, does not just emphasize Jesus's death—it also emphasizes his resurrection. Once again, the two should not be separated. When one is mentioned, the other is implied.[22] Nevertheless, it is helpful to see what each of the two accents so that we have a fuller appreciation. If Jesus's death focuses more on the forgiveness and cancellation of sins, then his resurrection focuses more on the victory and triumph over sins (e.g., 1 Cor 15:17). If his death purifies us, then his resurrection makes us righteous (e.g., Rom 4:25). Thus, the provision of righteousness and victory is highlighted more in his resurrection.[23]

In short, all the examples of authority, dominion, and victory of the Old Testament merely foreshadow the authority, dominion, and victory that Christ has over the ultimate problem—our sin. This war is won through the death and resurrection of the True David.

The Return of Christ (Rev 19:11–16)

The significance of his death and resurrection cannot be exhausted, so we reflect upon only one more passage as it is relevant to Jesus being the True

---

21. The verb for "**deliver**" is from the Greek *exaireō*, which is frequently used with military and/or political connotations (e.g., Josh 10:6, Judg 9:17, 1 Sam 7:3, 2 Kgs 17:39). The likely gloss from LSJ is "set free, deliver" (LSJ, s.v. "ἐξαιρέω," 581–82).

22. E.g., see the previously cited Calvin quote (*Institutes*, 2.16.13).

23. In addition to the premise above that the death and resurrection imply one another in the New Testament, Gaffin adduces the example of Rom 8:32–34: at first glance, it appears that justification is accomplished through the death of Christ (8:32–34a), but note the "more than that" (from the Greek *mallon*, 8:34b), which refers to "his resurrection with its enduring consequences" (8:34c) (*By Faith*, 107). This same logic and grammatical construction (*mallon*) are present in Rom 5:9–10.

David. The New Testament repeatedly mentions the exaltation of Christ after his death and resurrection, which has kingly connotations (e.g., Rom 1:3–4, Eph 1:20–23, Phil 2:8–11, Heb 1:3b–6). Some of these verses add the detail that the underlying role of Jesus's kingship is sonship: "I will be to him a father, and he shall be to me a son" (2 Sam 7:14a).

Hence, when Jesus returns, he does not come in the form of a vulnerable infant, born into a poor family. Rather, he returns as the rider on the white horse—in his glorious, exalted, and royal form. Revelation 19 provides the fullest description. Notice the royal adjectives in bold:

> Then I saw heaven opened, and behold, **a white horse!** The one sitting on it is called Faithful and True, and in righteousness **he judges and makes war.** His eyes are like a flame of fire, and on his head are many **diadems**, and he has a name written that no one knows but himself. He is **clothed in a robe** dipped in blood, and the name by which he is called is The Word of God. And **the armies of heaven**, arrayed in fine linen, white and pure, were following him on **white horses.** From his mouth comes **a sharp sword** with which **to strike down the nations**, and he will **rule them with a rod of iron.** He will tread the winepress of the fury of the wrath of God the Almighty. On his **robe** and on his **thigh** he has a name written, **King of kings** and **Lord of lords** (Rev 19:11–16; see also 1:12–16).[24]

This passage reveals that one of the reasons why Jesus returns as the rider on the white horse is to execute judgment and to destroy all sin as the True David (Rev 19:11, 15; see also Rev 19:17—20:15).[25] Jesus therefore finishes what he started with Satan. Earlier in his humiliation, Christ overcomes Satan's temptations (e.g., Luke 4:1–13); now in his exaltation, he delivers the fatal wound to his head (Gen 3:15, Rev 20:1–10). Revelation provides details about Satan that cue another inside joke. He is described not only as "the dragon, that ancient serpent" (Rev 20:2), but "the deceiver of the whole world" (Rev 12:9). If Adam succumbs to the lies of the serpent (Gen 3:1–8) and David secures temporary peace by slaying his serpentlike enemy who defies the name of God, then Jesus vanquishes "the dragon, that ancient serpent" to establish eternal peace. In all three, the enemy's tactic is

---

24. The word "**thigh**" in Greek is from *mēros*, which is where military officers would place their sword (e.g., Judg 3:16, 21; LSJ, s.v. "μηρός," 1129, citing *Ilias* 1.190 and *Odyssea* 11.231). See also Beale, *Book of Revelation*, 963.

25. In the ancient Near East and into the ancient Mediterranean, the common responsibilities of kings were to execute judgment and destroy enemies.

to distort, suppress, and reject the character and promises of God.[26] Only after executing judgment and destroying all evil does Jesus create all things new, which we will revisit shortly.

Thus, while the True Adam grants us the righteousness of Christ and the True Israel offers us the presence of God, the True David lavishes upon us the forgiveness and victory over sin. Of course none of these promises can be separated, but it is helpful to see how each promise punctuates certain facets of this gloriously infinite diamond of the person and work of Christ. More importantly, it is crucial to recognize that all these promises and blessings are secured by the death and resurrection of Christ.

SUMMARY

Just like any inside joke, the backstory is essential not only to understand the joke but to appreciate it. Otherwise we are forcing ourselves to laugh. We might be able to look the part, but eventually it becomes taxing. In many ways, this illustrates some of the frustrations of our own engagement with God's word and life in the gospel. This is especially true because of the Organism of Scripture: there is a significant unity despite the diversity of books, contexts, genres, and other aspects—all of which are grounded, saturated, and culminating in Christ.

Hence, this chapter explains the importance of intertextuality and provides several examples of how to apply it. It is important first to understand and appreciate the base passage. Only then should we look to see if there is a necessary backstory. If so, then we must reflect upon the similarities and—more importantly—the differences between the base passage and the backstory.

In the first example of this chapter, Luke portrays Jesus as the True Adam. Unlike Adam, the odds are heavily stacked against Jesus, yet his righteousness prevails. Moreover, this righteousness is (1) the epitome of all examples of righteousness, (2) necessary for the efficacy of his death, (3) imputed to his people, and (4) the image to which all his people are being conformed by the Holy Spirit.

---

26. We cannot unpack all the connections here. For instance, the Greek word for serpent, *ophis* (Rev 12:9, 20:2), is the same one used in Gen 3:1. Note also the "bronze serpent" account with Moses (Num 21:9), where the Hebrew bronze, *nechshet*, is used in 1 Sam 17:5 (*bis*), 6, 38. Additionally, the Greek word for devil, *diabolos* (Luke 4:2; Rev 12:9, 20:2), primarily means "slanderer" (LSJ, s.v. "διάβολος," 390).

The second example is Jesus as the True Israel. Where Israel disregards God's presence, Jesus is faithful to this privilege. He not only relishes in God's presence but has full authority to be there and to bring others with him. As a result of dwelling in God's holiness, where nobody could have ever imagined, his people can embody their God-given identity and become his witnesses.

Lastly, we see Jesus as the True David. His kingly authority is expressed through lowliness. Although this is unexpected, such meekness is prophesied centuries before Jesus's birth and is baked into his genealogy. As much as Jesus is the humble king, his triumph over sin is decisive. In his now-resurrected state, he shares his righteousness and victory with his people.

As mentioned earlier, when Jesus returns, he appears in the glorious and exalted state as the rider on the white horse, not only to judge and eradicate sin completely but to create the new heavens and the new earth. We get a picture of this in the final chapters of Scripture (Rev 21–22). Due to space limitations, we can only reflect upon two details in this vision of the new creation that are relevant to the questions raised in chapter 1.

The first question was why God comments that all his work in the original creation is "good" or "very good" except for day two. Day two is when God separates the heavenly realm from the earthly. This question is answered artistically in the closing chapters of Scripture, forming the ultimate inclusio—God finally converges these two realms so that his dwelling place is the same as that of his people. In the new creation, as much as we forever maintain the CREATOR-creature Distinction in reverence, God has done the unthinkable: "Behold, the dwelling place of God is with man. He will dwell with them, and they will be his people, and God himself will be with them as their God" (Rev 21:3b).

While Scripture begins with the CREATOR-creature Distinction, it ends with the wildest plot twist. The independent CREATOR, who has no need for his creation, not only condescends but incarnates as his own creation—despite humanity's perpetual rebellion. Moreover, Christ unites his people to himself so that their dwelling place is that of God's.[27] What is

---

27. Although this vision is multifaceted, "the figurative point of all the multiple pictures of end-time blessings is interpreted at the conclusion of v 7 to be *God's presence with his people*"; here it is through the metaphor of sonship, which connects to what we saw earlier about Jesus as the True Adam, the True Israel, and the True David. Thus, "Christ is still God's unique, divine son, but those whom he represents receive the privileges of his sonship." Beale, *Book of Revelation*, 1058; italics added. To be clear, there is still a

Christ as the Epitome of All Examples

astonishing is that this was in the mind of God from the opening verses of Scripture (thus, no comment on day two).[28] What makes this possible? As indicated below, it is the incarnation, life, *death*, *resurrection*, ascension, and return of Christ—the center of which should be obvious by now: his *death* and *resurrection*.

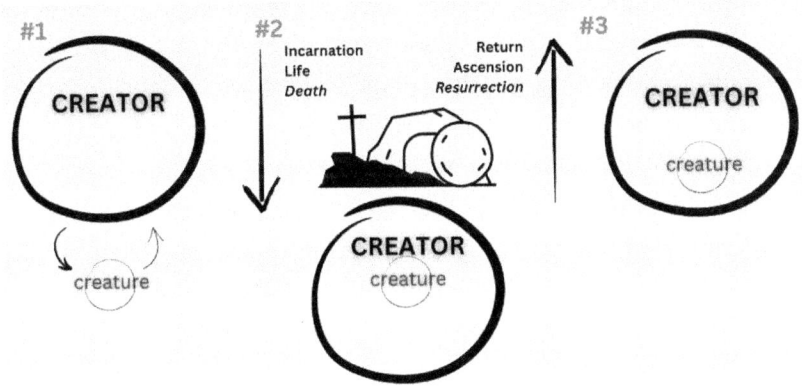

Additionally, we finally see the tree of life again in this vision (Rev 22:2). As observed earlier, God did not destroy it (Gen 3:22–24) but instead preserved it so that it can now be available for his people.

Indeed, Scripture is the best story ever told. Not only because it is real and riveting but because all roads are grounded, saturated, and culminating in Christ alone. The purpose of this book is to help us behold this truth more consistently as we engage in Scripture and consequently as we live life. This should have profound implications not only in our personal devotions but in the way we teach Scripture and minister the gospel. As a result, his people will glory in the death and resurrection of Christ in an organic and meaningful way, living happily—nay, joyfully—ever after.

QUESTIONS FOR REFLECTION AND PRAYER

a. As much as the characters of the Old Testament function as a spiritual mirror to us, Christ has shattered that mirror and given us a new identity in him. More specifically, through his death and resurrection, he has forgiven us all our sins, imputed his righteousness to us, and

---

distinction between CREATOR and creature despite this glorious union.

28. Passages like Eph 1:3–12 reveal that this was part of God's eternal will.

conforms us so that we can embody that righteousness in our everyday life. How has the Spirit been using these truths to edify you?

b. Among many other blessings that Christ has secured for us, this chapter demonstrates that Christ has made us righteous (as the True Adam), given us access to God's most holy presence (as the True Israel), and granted us ultimate victory while empathizing with us (as the True David). Which of these resonate(s) with you and why?

c. What does it mean to you that all of Scripture—from beginning to end—is about God's willingness to share his presence with us, and that he accomplishes this the way that he does?

d. How has this chapter (and the book overall) helped you engage in God's word as it is written (i.e., a careful reading) and intended (i.e., seeing the death and resurrection of Christ organically and meaningfully)? If not already, how might you see this impact spilling into the way you "read life"?

Conclusion: From and To Christ

THIS BOOK SOUGHT TO show how seeing Scripture as it is written and intended helps us to behold Jesus Christ, the gospel, and its implication. More specifically, we saw a particular sequence of biblical principles in the opening chapters of Genesis that repeats throughout Scripture: the CREATOR-creature Distinction, the Problem of Sin, and the Organism of Scripture. This book provides an explanation of these biblical principles, examples of applying them, and how-to steps for further application. As a result, the glory and relevance of the death and resurrection of Christ emerge organically and meaningfully. In short, all of Scripture reveals Jesus Christ, his gospel, and its implications.

At the same time, Christ, his gospel, and its implications are the very means that enable us to see all of Scripture as it is written and intended. This dynamic can send some of us down rabbit holes about the impossibility of exegesis and hermeneutics. Is a salvific relationship with Christ the chicken or the egg of engaging with Scripture? Indeed, this is a devastating problem. Because of the Problem of Sin, we distort everything, including God's word. So to return to the question, the answer is simply "Yes" and "Amen" (2 Cor 1:20). As much as Scripture reveals Christ, it is Christ who enables us to receive Scripture. In short, our engagement with Scripture is utterly dependent upon the very Jesus whom it reveals.

Thus, more than anything, I hope that this book encourages us not only to desire Christ but to depend on him. Prayer before, during, and after reading Scripture is a must and a delight. Because of the death and resurrection of Christ, we have the permanent dwelling of his Spirit who is bringing to remembrance his teachings (John 14:26), conforming us to the mind of Christ (1 Cor 2:16), and giving us the strength to understand and live according to what Christ has accomplished for us (Eph 3:16–19). There are countless instances where none of these promises feel real, and we see the limitations of our abilities and the depth and range of our sin. But our hope is never in our feelings or our abilities or our own righteousness. Instead our confidence is exclusively in Christ alone.

In short, only because he has died and resurrected for us and we died and resurrected with him (indicatives), we can place our full trust (imperative) in the certainty of all the promises in Scripture (fulfillment), which are about (wait for it) . . . his death and resurrection (Luke 24:44–46; 1 Cor 2:2, 15:3–4; Col 1:28). The circle is not to be avoided but embraced. "For 'in him we live and move and have our being'" (Acts 17:28). Or in the words of Jesus, he is "the Alpha and the Omega, the first and the last, the beginning and the end" (Rev 22:13).

APPENDIX

The Writings and the Prophets

DUE TO SPACE LIMITATIONS, we have not applied the threefold approach of the CREATOR-creature Distinction, Problem of Sin, and the Organism of Scripture to the Writings or the Prophets of the Old Testament. As beneficial as this approach is for other parts of Scripture, the approach might be most relevant for these portions Scripture. Without factoring these principles consistently, we are at the risk of misunderstanding the Writings and the Prophets. So this appendix provides a starting point for how to apply the threefold approach to these Old Testament books.

THE WRITINGS

The Writings or the wisdom literature comprises Job, Psalms, Proverbs, Ecclesiastes, and Song of Songs. We cannot summarize the introductory characteristics of these books, so this section seeks only to apply the threefold approach.[1]

---

1. Wisdom is difficult to define as a genre. Most include only Job, Proverbs, and Ecclesiastes. For the purposes of providing an introductory understanding and including all the books of the Old Testament in this book, I am grouping these five books together as wisdom literature or the Writings. For more extensive introductions to the wisdom literature, see Bartholomew, *Old Testament Wisdom Literature*; Longman, *Fear of the Lord*.

Appendix

The CREATOR-Creature Distinction

All these books urge their hearers to fear the LORD. Why? Not primarily because he is holy and therefore rightfully demands reverence but because the independent CREATOR is the source of all wisdom. Thus, in order to understand and live according to wisdom, one must depend on the LORD. Although God has no need, he generously bestows his wisdom upon those who trust him.

Wisdom, however, can look very different depending on the situation. Hence, each of the five books, while they overlap in many ways, focuses on a different dynamic of life. Roughly speaking, Job highlights fearing the LORD in the sufferings of life, Psalms in the emotions of life, Proverbs in the complexities of life, Ecclesiastes in the futility of life, and Song of Songs in the romance of life.

The Problem of Sin

Fearing the LORD and living according to his wisdom are difficult, not because of the different dynamics of life. Rather, the ultimate difficulty is the Problem of Sin. Whether it is the sin-fallen world, the sinners who are making the writers' lives difficult, or the sin of the writers themselves, fearing the LORD consistently is impossible. Humanity is continually distorting, suppressing, and rejecting God's character or promises. Hence, it is impossible to live perfectly according to his wisdom. It is from the ultimate issue of resisting the CREATOR-creature Distinction that a host of problems are expressed throughout the wisdom literature.

The Organism of Scripture

Earlier in chapter 2, we learned that prior to the New Testament, all of the Old Testament, including the wisdom literature, orbits around the Torah. With the New Testament, we see that not only does Christ fulfill all of the Torah but that all of Scripture has been orbiting around him. We also saw in the introduction that Christ says that all of Scripture points specifically to his death and resurrection. So the diagram and table below provide a sample of how each of these books can deepen our appreciation for the death and resurrection of Christ. However, each book does not highlight the death and resurrection equally.[2] So in the table, I put in **bold** what is the focus of the book and in *italics* what is more in the background of the book.

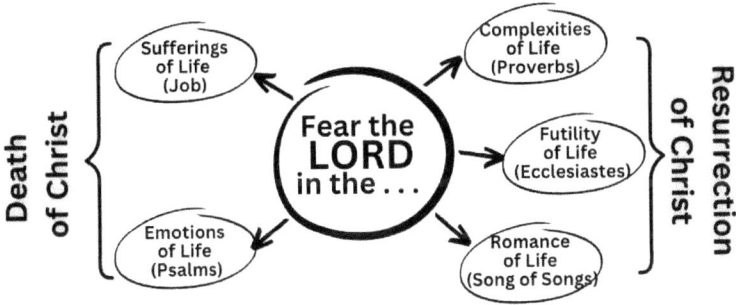

Book	Death of Christ	Resurrection of Christ
Job	**As much as Job is blameless and seeks to fear the LORD in his suffering, he falls short. Only Christ was perfectly sinless and submitted fully to the Father through the sufferings that he unjustly endured in order to save his people.**	*His resurrection declares that Christ was absolutely sinless and perfectly righteous in his life and death.*
Psalms	**Christ trusted the Father flawlessly in the midst of the range and depth of emotions, most of which were from his sufferings to rescue his people.**	*His resurrection proves that he is the anointed one, the Son of God, and the fulfillment of the Davidic covenant. Therefore, Christ secured eternal victory and ultimate peace for his people.*
Proverbs	*Christ suffered the consequences of his people living a life of folly because they refused to fear the LORD.*	**His resurrection proclaims that Christ perfectly feared the Father by living according to his wisdom despite the complexities of his life.**
Ecclesiastes	*All of God's precious creation is marred by futility and vanity because of humanity's sin—the consequences of such sin were satisfied by the death of Christ for his people.*	**The resurrected Christ inaugurates the new creation, enabling his people to be a new creation in him. Futility and vanity will therefore be vanquished.**
Song of Songs	*Christ took no shortcuts to redeem his bride, which includes his sufferings to sanctify and cleanse his bride.*	**The resurrected Christ consummates the marital covenant between himself and his people so that they can enjoy holistic union with him forever.**

2. See n. 21 in chapter 2 about how the death and resurrection entail one another.

APPENDIX

THE PROPHETS

The Prophets refer to the seventeen prophetic books of the Old Testament. These are divided by the five longer books known as the Major Prophets (Isaiah, Jeremiah and Lamentations, Ezekiel, and Daniel) and the twelve shorter known as the Minor Prophets (Hosea to Malachi). As summarized in chapter 5, these books were written across centuries, documenting God's countless attempts to warn Israel of their sin and to remind them of his trustworthiness. Israel, however, responds with recalcitrance. Thus, the language in the Prophets can be quite strong.[3]

The CREATOR-Creature Distinction

Many of us can get lost in the graphic language of the Prophets. It is therefore important to be reminded of the background of God's continual attempt to restore his relationship with Israel, only to be perpetually rejected. More fundamentally, everything in the Prophets is in the context of the CREATOR-creature Distinction. God is the independent CREATOR who graciously condescends, reveals, and covenants with Israel. He is absolute in his sovereignty and power. Hence, Israel's dependence on idols and political alliances is even more foolish and offensive.

The Problem of Sin

Another reason for the seemingly harsh language in the Prophets is that despite God's willingness to provide for his people, his people continually reject him. The Prophets are another example of God going out of his way to maintain the covenant despite Israel's continual defiance. He raises and sends prophet after prophet, only for them to be rejected—some of whom are even killed. If the prophets are speaking God's word that can save Israel, then why would Israel reject them? The fundamental reason for this is the Problem of Sin: Israel distorts, suppresses, and ultimately rejects God's character and promises.

---

3. For a more comprehensive introduction to the Prophets, see Paul House, "Introduction to the Prophetic Books," in Grudem et al., *Understanding the Big Picture*, 62–77; Tully, *Reading the Prophets*.

The Writings and the Prophets

The Organism of Scripture

Despite Israel's stubbornness, God nonetheless makes promises (thus more indicative-imperative-fulfillment triads). A couple of these promises are some of the most important ones in all of Scripture and are expressed with the most forceful language. They are also two of the more prominent themes throughout the Prophets: judgment of sin and promise of salvation.

One of the ways that the judgment of sin is described is through metaphors like afflictions and defeat, suffering and humiliation, and the exile. Similarly for the promise of salvation, the prophets use other metaphors that can be represented by things like the new covenant, new temple, and new creation. Both the judgment of sin and promise of salvation are often associated with the "day of the Lord."[4] As we should be able to guess by now, all these themes have been hinted since Gen 3 and are fulfilled in Christ—especially his death and resurrection. The diagram and table below show how these promises and themes can enrich our appreciation for the death and resurrection of Christ.

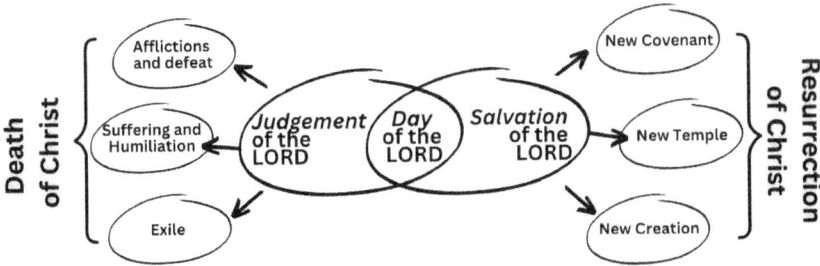

Image	Death and Resurrection of Christ
Afflictions and Defeat	As horrific as the afflictions and defeat, suffering and humiliation, and exile that Israel experienced were, they are merely a glimpse into the sufferings that Christ endured to save his people—all of which culminated in his **death**.
Suffering and Humiliation	
Exile	
New Covenant	All the glorious promises are secured by Christ through his **resurrection**: upon his **resurrection**, his people enjoy the firstfruit benefits of the new covenant, new temple, and new creation; at his return when his people are fully resurrected, Christ will fully consummate all these promises.
New Temple	
New Creation	

---

4. For further details on the "day of the Lord" from the Prophets, see J. D. Barker, "Day of the Lord," in Boda and McConville, *Prophets*, 132–43.

APPENDIX

CONCLUSION

While the resources cited in this appendix can help us appreciate the particularities of the Writings and the Prophets (i.e., reading Scripture as it is *written*), this appendix briefly provides a starting point for applying the threefold approach so that we can see how these Old Testament books are ultimately grounded, saturated, and culminating in Christ alone—especially his death and resurrection (i.e., reading Scripture as it is *intended*).

Glossary

Covenant: an intentional relationship based on shared experience that has stipulated expectations, promises, and consequences. *Covenants* are especially prevalent in the ancient Near East. Scripture is an expression of God's *covenant* with his people.

Covenantal/Iterative Flow: this concept helps us understand the *Organism of Scripture*. There is a flow or a recurring pattern throughout Scripture where are countless triads of *indicatives-imperatives-fulfillment*. Indicatives are facts or completed actions that flow into *imperatives* (commands). In Scripture, imperatives are not only commands but invitations to live according to indicatives. *Fulfillment* is whether indicatives have been trusted and imperatives have been followed. In Scripture, these triads are repeatedly broken until Christ arrives to fulfill them perfectly for his people.

CREATOR-creature Distinction: the first biblical principle of the threefold approach that we find in Scripture. This principle reminds us that God is the independent CREATOR who is the source of everything good. Though he has no need for anything, he graciously condescends, reveals, and covenants with humanity; humanity is the dependent creation who is to respond to God's grace with trust, obedience, and adoration.

Inclusio: a literary device to show the cohesion of a section of a text, usually to highlight the importance of the concept that frames that section.

Intertextuality: a relation between texts. This is especially prominent in Scripture where there are countless instances of portions of Scripture referring to other portions.

Glossary

Literary Flow: this concept helps us to understand the *Organism of Scripture*. All of Scripture is interconnected. Prior to Jesus Christ, all of the Old Testament orbits around the Torah. In Christ, not only is the entirety of the Old Testament fulfilled, but we learn that all of Scripture actually orbits around Christ. The Old Testament anticipates Christ while the New Testament expounds the significance of Christ.

Narrative: a genre where information is conveyed through a story. Thus, the basic elements of a story are present in narrative (e.g., plot, characters, setting, conflict, etc.).

Organism of Scripture: the third biblical principle of the threefold approach that we find in Scripture. This principle reminds us that all of Scripture is interconnected, orbiting around Jesus Christ, especially his death and resurrection. In order to understand the *Organism of Scripture* better, it is helpful to know the *Literary Flow* and the *Covenantal/Iterative Flow* of Scripture.

Problem of Sin: the second biblical principle of the threefold approach that we find in Scripture. This principle reminds us that the ultimate problem for the characters in Scripture as well as us readers is that we distrust God by distorting, suppressing, and/or rejecting God's character or promises.

Bibliography

Arnold, Bill T. *Genesis*. New Cambridge Bible Commentary. Cambridge: Cambridge University Press, 2009.
Arnold, Bill T., and H. G. M. Williamson, eds. *Dictionary of the Old Testament: Historical Books*. Downers Grove, IL: IVP Academic, 2005.
Bartholomew, Craig G. *Old Testament Wisdom Literature: A Theological Introduction*. Downers Grove, IL: IVP Academic, 2011.
Bartholomew, Craig G., and Michael W. Goheen. *The Drama of Scripture: Finding Our Place in the Biblical Story*. Grand Rapids: Baker Academic, 2004.
Bavinck, Herman. *Our Reasonable Faith*. Grand Rapids: Eerdmans, 1956.
———. *Reformed Dogmatics*. Edited by John Bolt. Translated by John Vriend. 4 vols. Grand Rapids: Baker Academic, 2003.
Beale, G. K. *The Book of Revelation: A Commentary on the Greek Text*. New International Greek Testament Commentary. Grand Rapids: Eerdmans, 1999.
———. *Handbook on the New Testament Use of the Old Testament: Exegesis and Interpretation*. Grand Rapids: Baker Academic, 2012.
Beale, G. K., and D. A. Carson. *Commentary on the New Testament Use of the Old Testament*. Grand Rapids: Baker Academic, 2007.
Block, Daniel I. *Covenant: The Framework of God's Grand Plan of Redemption*. Grand Rapids: Baker Academic, 2021.
Boda, Mark J., and J. Gordon McConville, eds. *Dictionary of the Old Testament: Prophets*. Downers Grove, IL: IVP Academic, 2012.
Bovon, François. *Luke 1: A Commentary on the Gospel of Luke 1:1—9:50*. Hermeneia. Minneapolis: Fortress, 2002.
———. *Luke 3: A Commentary on the Gospel of Luke 19:28—24:53*. Hermeneia. Minneapolis: Fortress, 2012.
Brock, Cory C., and N. Gray Sutanto. *Neo-Calvinism: A Theological Introduction*. Bellingham, WA: Lexham Academic, 2022.
Calvin, John. *Institutes of the Christian Religion*. Edited by John T. McNeill. Translated by Ford Lewis Battles. 2 vols. Rev. ed. Louisville: Westminster John Knox, 2006.
Childs, Brevard S. *The Book of Exodus: A Critical, Theological Commentary*. Old Testament Library. Rev. ed. Louisville: Westminster John Knox Press, 2004.
Clines, David J. A., ed. *Dictionary of Classical Hebrew*. 9 vols. Sheffield: Sheffield Phoenix, 1993–2016.
Clowney, Edmund P. *Preaching Christ in All of Scripture*. Wheaton, IL: Crossway, 2003.

Bibliography

Crowe, Brandon D. *The Last Adam: A Theology of the Obedient Life of Jesus in the Gospels.* Grand Rapids: Baker Academic, 2017.

———. *Why Did Jesus Live a Perfect Life? The Necessity of Christ's Obedience for Our Salvation.* Grand Rapids: Baker Academic, 2021.

Davies, W. D., and Dale C. Allison. *A Critical and Exegetical Commentary on the Gospel According to Saint Matthew.* 3 vols. International Critical Commentary. Edinburgh: T&T Clark, 1988.

Dawson, Nancy S., et al. *All the Genealogies of the Bible: Visual Charts and Exegetical Commentary.* Grand Rapids: Zondervan Academic, 2023.

Gaffin, Richard B., Jr. *By Faith, Not by Sight: Paul and the Order of Salvation.* London: Paternoster, 2006.

———. *Resurrection and Redemption: A Study in Paul's Soteriology.* Rev. ed. Phillipsburg, NJ: P&R, 1987.

Goldingay, John. *Genesis.* Baker Commentary on the Old Testament. Grand Rapids: Baker Academic, 2020.

Goldsworthy, Graeme. *Gospel-Centered Hermeneutics: Foundations and Principles of Evangelical Biblical Interpretation.* Downers Grove, IL: IVP Academic, 2006.

Grudem, Wayne, et al., eds. *Understanding the Big Picture of the Bible: A Guide to Reading the Bible Well.* Wheaton, IL: Crossway, 2012.

Hendel, Ronald S. *Genesis 1–11: A New Translation with Introduction and Commentary.* Anchor Yale Bible. New Haven: Yale University Press, 2024.

Hess, Richard S. "The Genealogies of Genesis 1–11 and Comparative Literature." *Biblica* 70 (1989) 241–54.

Johnson, Dennis E. *Him We Proclaim: Preaching Christ from All the Scriptures.* Phillipsburg, NJ: P&R, 2007.

Koehler, Ludwig, et al. *The Hebrew and Aramaic Lexicon of the Old Testament.* 3rd ed. Leiden: Brill, 2001.

Kruger, Michael J., ed. *A Biblical-Theological Introduction to the New Testament: The Gospel Realized.* Wheaton, IL: Crossway, 2016.

Kuyper, Abraham. *Encyclopedia of Sacred Theology: Its Principles.* Translated by J. Hendrik de Vries. New York: Scribner's Sons, 1898.

Liddell, Henry George, et al. *A Greek-English Lexicon.* 9th ed. Oxford: Clarendon, 1996.

Lillback, Peter A., ed. *Seeing Christ in All of Scripture: Hermeneutics at Westminster Theological Seminary.* Philadelphia: Westminster Seminary, 2016.

Long, V. Philips. *1 and 2 Samuel: An Introduction and Commentary.* Tyndale Old Testament Commentaries 8. Downers Grove, IL: IVP Academic, 2020.

Longman, Tremper, III. *The Fear of the Lord Is Wisdom: A Theological Introduction to Wisdom in Israel.* Grand Rapids: Baker Academic, 2017.

Luz, Ulrich. *Matthew: A Commentary.* Minneapolis: Augsburg, 1989.

Meyers, Carol L. *Exodus.* New Cambridge Bible Commentary. Cambridge: Cambridge University Press, 2005.

Milgrom, Jacob. *Leviticus 1–16: A New Translation with Introduction and Commentary.* Anchor Bible 3. New York: Doubleday, 1991.

Morgan, Teresa. *Roman Faith and Christian Faith: Pistis and Fides in the Early Roman Empire and Early Churches.* Oxford: Oxford University Press, 2015.

Muether, John R. *Cornelius Van Til: Reformed Apologist and Churchman.* Phillipsburg, NJ: P&R, 2008.

Murray, John. *Redemption Accomplished and Applied.* Rev. ed. Grand Rapids: Eerdmans, 2015.

Bibliography

Poythress, Vern S. *Interpreting Eden: A Guide to Faithfully Reading and Understanding Genesis 1–3*. Wheaton, IL: Crossway, 2019.

———. *In the Beginning Was the Word: Language—A God-Centered Approach*. Wheaton, IL: Crossway, 2009.

———. *Reading the Word of God in the Presence of God: A Handbook for Biblical Interpretation*. Wheaton, IL: Crossway, 2016.

Ridderbos, Herman. *Paul: An Outline of His Theology*. Rev. ed. Grand Rapids: Eerdmans, 1997.

Smith, Christian, and Melinda Lundquist Denton. *Soul Searching: The Religious and Spiritual Lives of American Teenagers*. New York: Oxford University Press, 2005.

Stol, Marten. *Women in the Ancient Near East*. Boston: De Gruyter, 2016.

Strawn, Brent A., ed. *The Oxford Encyclopedia of the Bible and Law*. Oxford: Oxford University Press, 2015.

Tully, Eric J. *Reading the Prophets as Christian Scripture: A Literary, Canonical, and Theological Introduction*. Reading Christian Scripture. Grand Rapids: Baker Academic, 2022.

Van Pelt, Miles V., ed. *A Biblical-Theological Introduction to the Old Testament: The Gospel Promised*. Wheaton, IL: Crossway, 2016.

Verrett, Brian A. *The Serpent in Samuel: A Messianic Motif*. Eugene, OR: Resource, 2020.

Vos, Geerhardus. *Biblical Theology: Old and New Testaments*. Rev. ed. Grand Rapids: Eerdmans, 1968.

Waltke, Bruce K. *Genesis: A Commentary*. Grand Rapids: Zondervan, 2021.

Walton, John H. *Ancient Near Eastern Thought and the Old Testament: Introducing the Conceptual World of the Hebrew Bible*. Grand Rapids: Baker Academic, 2006.

———. *The Lost World of Genesis One: Ancient Cosmology and the Origins Debate*. Downers Grove, IL: IVP Academic, 2009.

Watkin, Christopher. *Biblical Critical Theory: How the Bible's Unfolding Story Makes Sense of Modern Life and Culture*. Grand Rapids: Zondervan Academic, 2022.

Wilson, Robert R. *Genealogy and History in the Biblical World*. Yale Near Eastern Researches 7. New Haven: Yale University Press, 1977.

Yuh, Jason N., ed. *Kingdom Manifesto: Meditations on the Gospel of Matthew*. Wycliffe Studies in Gospel, Church, and Culture. Eugene, OR: Wipf & Stock, 2021.

www.ingramcontent.com/pod-product-compliance
Lightning Source LLC
Chambersburg PA
CBHW051106160426
43193CB00010B/1336